PSALMS

FOR

LIVING

A Study in Selected Psalms

PSALMS
FOR
LIVING

A Study in Selected Psalms

WALLIS C. METTS

ACCENT ON LIFE
BIBLE CURRICULUM

ADULT STUDENT
Bible Study Guide

This Bible Study Guide is a part of a ten-year adult curriculum designed to assist you in making the entire Bible your Guide for daily living.

Based on a course originally
written by Robert P. Lightner

Wallis C. Metts/Author
James T. Dyet/Executive Editor
Robert L. Mosier/Publisher

Accent on Life Bible Curriculum
Accent-B/P Publications
12100 W. Sixth Avenue
P.O. Box 15337
Denver, Colorado 80215

ISBN 0-916406-85-7

CONTENTS

IN ALL PROBABILITY. . .

One of your favorite and most familiar passages of Scripture is Psalm 23. You may have memorized it some years ago to earn a prize in Sunday School or VBS. Or perhaps you remember seeing it on a plaque in your grandmother's living room. No matter how or where you first heard it, no doubt the Twenty-Third Psalm has touched your heart many times.

King David, the famous author of the Twenty-Third Psalm and many other psalms, had a way of speaking that could reach almost anyone in almost any situation. When you're down in the dumps, his writings can cheer you up. When you're excited because of a special blessing or opportunity, the Psalms express the joy you feel. When you have strayed from God's will, the Psalms gently nudge you back into the right way.

These sacred writings have been used for centuries in the Jews' worship of Jehovah. Put to music, they offer praise to Jehovah; they express sorrow over sin; they request God's protection and blessing. And although they are ancient, they are new each time we read them.

It is obvious that David and the other authors of the Psalms were about as "human" as anyone could be. They experienced the same disappointments, the same frustrations, the same joy, the same exhaustion, the same relief, the same agony, the same defeats that we experience all through our lives. These men were not set on a hill somewhere away from persecution, without enemies and free from the troubles life brings. They were in the midst of battles; they struggled with temptation; sometimes they even felt God had deserted them. But they also found out that even though life might deliver them what they considered to be a bad deal, they could turn to the omnipotent One, the One who promised to guide them and protect them in every aspect of their lives. Granted, they failed the Lord many times, just as we do. But they were forgiven and restored to victory when they confessed their sin. And they offered advice to us no matter what our station in life, no matter where we are, no matter what our problems may be.

In Psalms 16; 22; 24; and 72, we read some prophecies of the coming King—the Lord Jesus Christ. We see Him in the agony of the cross and then in the glory of His kingdom. What encouragement to keep on serving Christ in the face of trials and troubles!

In Psalm 19, David points out the value of the Word of God. He tells us it is sweeter than honey, worth more than gold; it is enlightening, pure, profitable, enduring.

In Psalms 42 and 43 the psalmist expresses what we all have felt at one time or another—that inexplicable thirst for something more than we have found—that desire that only God can meet. But then, three times in these two psalms David affirms that God alone brings hope and health, and for this reason we need not despair, but should praise Him continually.

Psalm 40 gives us a striking picture of our salvation and Christian life; Psalm 91 expresses the wonder of God's protection of His own; Psalms 15 and 103 talk about worship, that great privilege of every child of God.

Perhaps the most emotional of all the psalms is Psalm 51, where David pours out his soul before God in contrition over his great sin of adultery and consequent murder. He confesses that he has sinned, and that he needs the forgiveness only God can give. He pleads with God to restore the joy he has lost, and promises to tell others of God's glory. What one of us has not experienced this at some time in his life?

There are many other psalms, with many messages—each different from the others. But you can be sure that at any given time, in any situation, the Lord can, and will, speak to you through one of these blessed poems.

Why not sit down right now, and begin reading through the book of Psalms? You will receive abundant blessing, encouragement, and strength. And you will rejoice at the wonderful message the Lord has given you.

Surveying the Psalms

1

LESSON SCRIPTURE
Psalm 1; Luke 24:44

RELATED SCRIPTURE
Joshua 1:7-9; Psalms 95; 98; Acts 1:15-20;
13:26-33; Ephesians 5:15-21; Colossians
3:12-17

LESSON AIM
To love God's Word; to meditate upon it;
to obey its precepts.

LEARN BY HEART
"Blessed is the man that walketh not in the
counsel of the ungodly, nor standeth in the
way of sinners, nor sitteth in the seat of the
scornful. But his delight is in the law of the
Lord; and in his law doth he meditate day
and night" (Psalm 1:1,2).

EVERY DAY WITH THE WORD

STUDENT'S NOTEBOOK

This column is for the student who desires additional study of the lesson theme.

Monday	The Lord's righteousness	Psalm 72
Tuesday	The Lord's greatness	Psalm 89
Wednesday	The Lord's patience	Psalm 106
Thursday	The Lord's goodness	Psalm 107
Friday	The Lord's deliverance	Psalm 116
Saturday	The Lord's creation	Psalm 148
Sunday	The Lord's faithfulness	Psalm 41

LESSON PREPARATION

Psalm 7:17

As we begin our study of the book of Psalms, you will see two things very clearly: the greatness of God and the infirmity of men. It is in this contrast that the Psalms invite us to worship God because He is so much greater than man. It is to

9

our advantage, then, to approach this study with a spirit of reverence and awe.

It is also wise to expect something from God to help us with our own personal needs. The Bible was written to reveal God to us because that is what we need. We cannot expect to deal realistically with life until we have a clear view of life, and that is impossible unless we have a clear view of God. As much as any other portion of Scripture, the Psalms reveal our needs and God's great capacity to meet those needs.

THE PSALMS—A MANIFOLD REVELATION OF GOD (Luke 24:44)

The value of the Bible is that it tells the truth about God and man. The human tendency is to gloss over sin, as the idealist does, or to glorify it, as the humanist does. The Bible does neither. It presents man exactly as he is. It paints the picture of his need, his sin and his utter dependence upon God. That is one of the reasons why we can be sure the Bible is the Word of God. No man, unaided by divine help, would ever have written it that way. In many of the passages in Psalms, for instance, we see the king of Israel, David, as he reveals his own absolutely erring condition. "I was shapen in iniquity," he says, "and in sin did my mother conceive me" (Psalm 51:5). In the Thirty-Eighth Psalm he cries because of the utter corruption of his own life and the effects of sin upon it. He was given unusual insight into the great spiritual dearth in man until he could cry out, "I acknowledge my transgressions; and my sin is ever before me" (Psalm 51:3).

An attitude of honesty and unbiased openness is also a good asset to us as we study the Bible.

At the same time, over against the dearth of strength in man he contrasts the absolute sufficiency of Jehovah. Nowhere are His attributes more clearly pictured or more highly exalted than in the Psalms.

For further study see Psalms 24:1,10; 47:2; 88:18; 89:11; 95:3; 103:19; 113:4.

He is seen as the source of joy: "Thou hast put gladness in my heart, more than in the time that their corn and their wine increased" (Psalm 4:7). He is the source of every good thing: "No good thing will he withhold from them that walk uprightly" (Psalm 84:11). He is the Creator: "When I consider thy heavens, the work of thy fingers, the moon and the stars, which thou hast ordained" (Psalm 8:3). He is eternal: "Before the mountains were brought forth, or ever thou hadst formed the earth and the world, even from everlasting to everlasting, thou art God" (Psalm 90:2). He is altogether faithful: "Thy mercy, O Lord, is in the heavens; and thy faithfulness reacheth unto the clouds" (Psalm 36:5).

This is a very small sampling of the passages in the Psalms which magnify the Person of God. When we study these magnificent overtures of praise to God, our hearts can be lifted toward Him.

Another unique contribution to our well-being is found in the Messianic passages. They can serve two purposes in our lives. First, they confirm the truth and accuracy of God's Word. Upon examining all the evidence, only a very foolish person would conclude that the Bible prophecies delivered by the Old Testament prophets, of whom David was one, were not true. The hundreds of details prophesied about and fulfilled in the life and death of Christ remove any room for chance fulfillment. God has proven His Word by

Some fulfilled prophecies from Psalms are: 2:7,8 with Matthew 3:17; 22:18 with Matthew 27:35; 22:7,8 with Luke 23:35; 69:4 with John 15:24,25;

His working in the nation of Israel and the life of His Son.

69:21 with Matthew 27:34; 34:20 with John 19:33,36

Second, the Psalms force upon our minds the full truth of who Jesus really is. He is without a doubt one with the Father, the Creator and sustainer of all life. The Psalmist, centuries before Christ's birth, heralded the glorious incarnation, the humiliating death, the victorious resurrection and the coming reign of our Lord Jesus Christ. A careful comparison of the Messianic Psalms and other old Testament references to Christ with the New Testament record of their fulfillment would erase any doubt from our minds that the Lord Jesus is indeed the one Lord, the Saviour of all who come to Him.

And so for our worship, for our assurance, for our confirmation and witness to others, the Psalms provide a remarkable source to learn about God and His Son.

THE PSALMS—A MIRROR OF REALITY ABOUT MAN (Psalm 1)

Scientists are finding that they know less and less about more and more. The most recent sensation is the discovery and speculation about mysterious ''black holes'' in the universe in which the force of gravity sucks in the mass of huge suns until they are condensed to the size of a golf ball. It is speculated that the resulting density is so great that its gravitational pull bends light rays until both light and time disappear. The fear is that, according to Einstein's theory, eventually these black holes will suck in the whole universe and that both reality and time will disappear.

See Revelation 6:14.

Reader's Digest, September, 1977.

One of the basic requirements for obtaining wisdom is to admit our need to know more.

I Timothy 6:3-5

It was the fact that God knew so much about him that held David in such awe (Psalm 139:17,18).

Hebrews 4:12

How much do you suppose we really know about the universe? If we gathered together all the known facts and weighed them against everything else there is to know, what do you think the percentage of what we know would be? One percent? Hardly. It would be far less.

How foolish, then, for us to let the "experts" and opinion-makers dictate to us what we ought to believe as if they knew everything. And we don't even have to go out in the universe to find a world of reality that they don't understand. For we haven't gone much farther in conquering the "inner space" of man than we have in conquering outer space. In fact, it seems that the more "enlightened" we become, the more our problems multiply.

The only accurate source of information about man is in God's Word. He is the One who made us, and He understands all about us. The only totally accurate picture of reality as it touches our lives is the one that God gives.

That is why God can give the promises of the first Psalm. He promises us that if we will refrain from the counsel of the ungodly, the way of sinners and the seat of the scornful we can avoid an unrealistic picture of life. On the other hand, if we meditate upon His Word, we will have a realistic view of life. We will be thinking the right thoughts, making the right decisions, and taking the right actions.

The media and the "experts" place their emphasis upon what we *have*. God says it is far more important to place our emphasis upon what we *are*. According to Proverbs 23:7, we are what we think. An action is impossible without a thought. The right kinds of thoughts always lead to the

13

right kinds of actions. It is only by structuring our thought life around the wisdom of God that we can hope to meet life's challenges successfully and come out victoriously. He gives us warnings and challenges along the way to program the right responses into our minds. He wants us to fear the consequences of evil and revere His commandments in order for us to make the right choices. That is why the fear of the Lord is called the beginning of wisdom (Proverbs 9:10).

God has given us a wonderful faculty called "imagination." It is the ability to picture things in our minds. We have something like a little screen in our minds in which a response calls forth a long forgotten picture in order for us to identify knowledge. We build this picture gallery with all our experiences. When something is unfamiliar to us, we always compare it to the things we see and hear that are familiar. That is how we learn.

According to Genesis 6:5, the total corruption of man's imagination was one of the factors that caused God to bring the flood upon the earth.

God has filled His Word with the right kinds of pictures. The Bible is written in concrete images that we can identify with. Meditation upon the Scriptures is the art of turning God's thought pictures over in our minds until they become a part of our hearts. We visualize what He is saying by applying it to our own lives and to those things with which we are familiar. As we do this, the Spirit of God is able to impress these principles and concepts home to us. They become a part of our living experience.

Note the imagery in Psalm 1: walking, standing, sitting, the tree, the rivers of water, the leaf, the fruit, and the chaff which the wind drives away.

When this becomes true in our lives, we are equipped to make the right choices when we are faced with two possible alternatives. In this way we will know God's will because His Word has been implanted into our minds. In Psalm 1 and in Joshua 1:8, God promises that this kind of activity

See Philippians 2:5-13.

will produce success and prosperity. After all, how can we miss if we are thinking the thoughts of the One who formed all things by His Word and founded the earth upon His wisdom? (See Romans 12:2; II Corinthians 10:4,5.)

Everybody nowadays wants "the real thing." But contrary to what we hear, "the real thing" is not a soft drink or a shampoo. Reality is pictured in God's Word. And we can only come to a realistic view of ourselves and the world around us by exposing ourselves to that living reality.

FOOD FOR THOUGHT

"The man who delights in God's Word. . . bringeth forth patience in the time of suffering, faith in the day of trial, and holy joy in the hour of prosperity. . . . Fruitfulness should be seasonable."—Charles Haddon Spurgeon

NOW TEST YOUR KNOWLEDGE

Answer true or false:
1. It is difficult to find any evidence that the Bible is divinely inspired.
2. The Bible reveals the glory of man and God.
3. King David was keenly aware that he was a sinner.
4. The most accurate source of information about life is the news.
5. Imagination is the ability to picture things in our minds.
6. Meditation is something Christians should avoid.
7. Any seeming fulfillment of Old Testament prophecy is merely coincidental.
8. God will bless those who make His Word of utmost importance in their lives.

LESSON SCRIPTURE
Psalm 99; 136; 139

RELATED SCRIPTURE
Psalms 34; 36; 86; 145; Acts 17:23-31;
Revelation 2:2,9,13; 3:1,8,15

2

LESSON AIM
To trust God to supply our needs.

LEARN BY HEART
"O Lord, thou hast searched me, and known me. Whither shall I go from thy spirit? or whither shall I flee from thy presence?" (Psalm 139:1,7).

EVERY DAY WITH THE WORD

Monday	His presence	Psalm 139:7-16
Tuesday	His goodness	Psalm 34
Wednesday	His greatness	Psalm 86
Thursday	His mercy	Psalm 136
Friday	His grace	Psalm 145
Saturday	His understanding	Psalm 147
Sunday	His knowledge	Psalm 139:1-6

STUDENT'S NOTEBOOK

This column is for the student who desires additional study of the lesson theme.

LESSON PREPARATION

It is a sobering fact to realize that God knows us better than anyone else knows us. Many of us are deluded into thinking somehow that God is not looking, that there are some things in our lives that He does not know about. In Psalm 139 the full realization of God's all-knowing eye was almost too much for David to comprehend. If we would think upon it, we would also be staggered by this thought.

The greatness of God is measured in part by His attributes. They describe the extent of His infinite superiority over us. But His greatness is also expressed in the passages that describe His goodness—His grace and mercy toward us. God knows all about us, including our deepest needs. And His perfect knowledge is matched by His abounding mercy.

THE ALL-KNOWING GOD
(Psalm 139)

It was a literal paradise, the most beautiful spot the world has ever known (Genesis 2:8-15). Sea creatures made their shimmering wake nearby where lush plant life gave beauty and food to every corner of the garden. The temperature was perfect. Everything the occupants needed was provided. No telephones, salesmen or social demands were around to complicate their lives, and yet Adam and Eve shrank from the minimal demands of their almost perfect environment to hide (Genesis 3:8). Their environment had not changed, but something had happened inside them. They were afraid. They were hiding from God. A deep sense of shame caused their consciences to recoil from the presence of the Holy One because they had disobeyed Him. And so it has been with every person since Eden (Romans 5:12).

The ways we hide are almost endless, but we all hide (see John 3:19,20). Some hide behind activities, some behind the praise of others. Others

The garden of Eden is a reminder that man's multiple problems arise, not from an imperfect environment, but from his own guilt and shame.

retreat in psychological regression. One of the favorite activities of men is to hide from God.

Perhaps that is why David expresses such wonder at his realization, expressed in Psalm 139, that he could not hide from God. Verse 1 expresses the idea that God has known everything there is to know about David. In verse 2, David declares that both his activities and thoughts are known of God. In 4, David is amazed that every word is heard by God. In verses 7-12, we are told that there is no place in all of creation where we are not seen, for God's eyes penetrate even the thick darkness. In verse 6, David cries out that such knowledge is beyond the limits of his understanding.

None of us can come to a full realization of what God's omniscience really means. This is readily seen in the fact that while we have an idea that His eye is upon us, we still do things that offend His holiness. We have a head knowledge of His omniscience, but our hearts keep looking for hiding places.

The moral relativism of our day has led many to be deluded into thinking that right and wrong are flexible guidelines that bend according to the shape of the circumstances. But the Bible teaches that there are moral *absolutes,* determined by the Judge of all the earth. And the sobering fact is that He needs no one to report to Him on the evidence. The witness is His own all-seeing eye. The Judge is looking all the time.

As sobering as this realization is, there is a comforting side to it as well. This thought is brought out in Psalm 139:13-18. The psalmist reminds us that each of us is made according to God's exact prescription (verses 13-16). This truth is borne out by the modern science of genet-

Modern Freudian psychology recognizes that guilt is one of our greatest hangups. Its error is in the remedy it proposes for that guilt. Rather than forgiveness, the Freudian solution is to change the standards in which it is imagined the "false" sense of guilt lies. Thus righteous standards are constantly dismissed as "puritanical" or "Victorian."

Jeremiah 6:15,16

Realizing this truth gives us an excellent

opportunity to accept the Creator's design and submit everything in our lives to Him.

ics. Studies of the human cell have shown us that the physical traits of each individual are locked in the particular characteristics of the chromosome cells. They are determined long before conception. This remarkable truth is given to us in verse 16, centuries before the geneticist ever had a microscope to look through. Read the verse carefully and thrill to the fact that an all-knowing God made you with an identity and appearance unlike anybody else who has ever lived. His infinite love and care for each of us as a unique individual is stamped vividly in our appearance. It is only a bitter and unthankful person who will reject that work of creative omniscience by comparing himself unfavorably with others.

God's care in prescribing and preserving our identity is shown in His plan for our redemption. It is each distinct individual that Christ died to save. He did not come to do away with that person (see John 3:17) but to save that individual. And we are told that in Heaven we will have a distinct identity that is shared only with Him (Revelation 2:17).

"Dying to self" does not mean that we get rid of the one whom God has created. He loved each one of us and sent His Son to die for us, therefore He is not trying to do away with us. To die to self means to separate ourselves from the kinds of selfish plans and ambitions that are contrary to God's will and therefore harmful to us.

In Psalm 139:19-24 David dares to expose his heart to God to examine his thoughts and determine that David is on God's side in the conflict between good and evil. We should also ask the Lord to "see if there be any wicked way" in us (verse 24), and confess the sin God reveals in us.

THE ALL-SUFFICIENT GOD
(Psalms 99; 136)

Picture a group of men lined up on the rim of a ravine, attempting to jump across to the other side. One by one they come up to the edge and make their attempt, and one by one they fall tragically to the rocks below. Some of them are able to jump just a short distance, others are able to jump almost all the way across. But none of them can make it to the other side. Here you have a picture of man's attempts to get to God through his own goodness. Some men are ''better'' than others, but all miss the mark of God's holiness (Romans 3:23).

We cannot even fully understand how holy God is, much less measure up to that holiness. In Psalm 99:1 we are told that God sits between the cherubim. A similar scene was too much for Isaiah in Isaiah 6:1-5. He fell prostrate before the Holy One, even as the Apostle John must have done on Patmos (Revelation 4:8-10).

In Psalm 99:2 we see God's exalted position in relationship to His people. We notice the holiness of His name in verse 3, even as in the model prayer (Matthew 6:9). In Psalm 99:5,9 we see that He is worthy of our worship.

The proper reaction to God's holiness is shown to us in this Psalm. In verse 1 we are told to tremble, verse 3 tells us to praise Him, verse 5 says we are to exalt Him and worship Him, and verse 6 tells us to call upon Him.

We can clearly see that we cannot hide from God, nor can we stand in the presence of His shining holiness and glory. What are we to do, then? The Scriptures teach that we are dependent upon His mercy. In the spirit of this age men often demand their rights. But we dare not do that with God. For if we received our rights in the presence of a holy God, severe judgment would befall us.

A customer once returned to the photographer

God is self-existent. Since He called everything into being, He is dependent upon no other entity or power for His existence and continuance. So unlike us, God is dependent upon nothing.

In recognizing the attributes of God, the only appropriate thing for His creatures to do is to worship Him and praise Him. Only in ascribing greatness to such lofty attributes can we grow in conformity to the image of the only perfect Person.

to pick up his proofs and was displeased with what he saw. When the customer complained that the proofs did not do him justice, the photographer replied, "What you need is not justice, but mercy!" When we see ourselves pictured in contrast to the holiness of God, "mercy" is our only plea.

Psalm 136 is that unusual Psalm in which each verse ends with the phrase, "For his mercy endureth forever." It is a Psalm given to us to encourage us to recognize God's mercy—*love in action* as God shows us His kindness and faithfulness.

Part of the Psalm reminds us of God's creative acts. It is within the scope of His mercy that He gives us the sunshine, the rain, the trees and all the other things we so often take for granted. And He gives these things freely to all, even to His enemies. The great scheme of nature makes possible the food chain, providing food for not only mankind but the beasts of the forest as well (verse 25; Psalm 104:14). Although God is often blamed for it, it is the sin of man that has forbidden this bounty to some people.

Somewhat harder to comprehend are the verses dealing with God's judgment upon the enemies of Israel (verses 15,17-20). We need to look at these in the broader context of God's plan of redemption. His plan was to single out the seed of Abraham to prove to the world that His Word was true and to provide the Saviour of the world. When Israel's enemies threatened to eliminate them, the only recourse for God was to fight for Israel in order to preserve the larger blessing.

Only God's mercy is able to meet our ultimate need. His great love recognized us as spiritually

The heart of unbelief is unthankful for the merciful benefits of God and focuses instead upon things which are imagined to be withheld. As in the garden of Eden, we ignore the other trees, so freely given, and desire the one tree that is forbidden. We live in an imperfect world, marred by our own sin, but somehow we imagine that God owes us a perfect world.

Genesis 12:1-3

helpless and completely undone. According to the second chapter of Ephesians, we were controlled by Satan, the god of this world (verse 2); in captivity to the desires of our own bodies (verse 3); and therefore cut off from God. But God reached out to us in mercy (Ephesians 2:4-7). His love responded to our need, His mercy reached out to us and His grace was given to us in full remedy for our sins.

We can praise Him when we realize that He not only knows our need, but is sufficient to provide everything we need. And we can trust Him because He is the only One who can discern our true needs and desires and perfectly provide for them (Psalm 37:4-6).

It is grace that characterizes the bountiful provision of our greatest need, salvation. It is God's greatest gift to us, who are so undeserving.

FOOD FOR THOUGHT

"He that has tasted the bitterness of sin fears to commit it, and he that hath felt the sweetness of mercy will fear to offend it."—Selected

Answer true or false:

1. Most of man's problems result from an imperfect environment.
2. David said that he understood everything about God's omniscience.
3. Right and wrong are determined by the circumstances.
4. Before we were born, God prescribed our appearance exactly the way He wanted it.
5. God's mercy causes the rain and the sunshine to fall upon both the just and the unjust.
6. Men often succeed in hiding from God.
7. The eye of the Lord is looking upon us all the time.
8. In Heaven we will have a distinct identity that will be shared only with God.
9. We should demand our rights.
10. Psalm 139 tells us of God's mercy.

God's Revelation to Us

3

LESSON SCRIPTURE
Psalm 19

RELATED SCRIPTURE
Romans 1; I Timothy 6:11-21; II Timothy 3:12-17; Psalm 119

LESSON AIM
To study God's Word.

LEARN BY HEART
"The law of the Lord is perfect, converting the soul: the testimony of the Lord is sure, making wise the simple" (Psalm 19:7).

EVERY DAY WITH THE WORD

Monday	Blessing	Psalm 119:1-24
Tuesday	Hope	Psalm 119:25-48
Wednesday	Comfort	Psalm 119:49-72
Thursday	Understanding	Psalm 119:73-104
Friday	Righteousness	Psalm 119:105-136
Saturday	Deliverance	Psalm 119:137-152
Sunday	Delight	Psalm 119:153-176

STUDENT'S NOTEBOOK

This column is for the student who desires additional study of the lesson theme.

LESSON PREPARATION

One day there was nothing but the triune God. He looked out upon the emptiness of nothing and commanded it to be something. The universe was born. Everything that is here is here because God commanded it to be. As strange as this may seem to us, it is the truth. The whole universe of created things is founded upon God's Truth, which is the only permanent reality. God spoke and it was done.

Hebrews 11:3

The material universe is here as a constant testimony of God's Truth. The punctuality of the heavenly bodies, the design and balance of nature, the beauty of creation—all reflect consistency and power of an eternal God.

GOD'S REVELATION IN THE WORLD
(Psalm 19:1-6)

A photographer points a little box toward the sunset and snaps the shutter open for a few seconds. Light floods in, activates some chemicals on a piece of plastic and makes an image. Later, we look at it and say, "Oh, what a beautiful sunset!" But it is not a sunset at all. It is only a piece of paper that has caught the reflected glory of a sunset.

An artist takes his brushes and arranges a certain chemical called paint upon a canvas in his skillful way. Again we say, "What a beautiful sunset!" But it is not a sunset. It is only an illusion. It is only the clever arranging of pigments which have imitated the glory of a sunset. Light, striking the surface of the different pigments, reflects back to us in such a way that it reminds us of a sunset. It is an image. But where does the light come from that makes the sunset, affects the film, reflects from the paint and makes all other visual reality possible?

When we trace that light all the way back to its source, we come to the inconceivable glory of the self-existent God. We are reminded of that in I Timothy 6:16: "Who only hath immortality, dwelling in the light which no man can approach unto; whom no man hath seen, nor can see: to whom be honour and power everlasting."

The person who only "believes what he sees" lives in a very limited world.

When Jesus said, "I am the light of the world," He meant it both figuratively and literally.

25

In Psalm 19, the psalmist reminds us that glory is reflected from the heavens and from every corner of creation to remind us of the God behind that glory. In verse 1 he writes, "The heavens declare the glory. . . and the firmament sheweth his handywork." God's glory shines from His Person, races through the galaxies, and when it diffuses in the atmosphere it lights up the earth to show us the handiwork of God. In this sense, David pictures the sun as a messenger bearing the glad tidings of the heavenly Bridegroom. Light appeared in the Genesis account of creation before the sun and the moon, because it comes directly from God. The Bible goes on to say the sun and moon were given to us as "signs." Actually, they are signposts pointing us toward the glory of God.

See Malachi 4:2, where the Messiah is called the Sun of righteousness.

We can picture nature as a giant screen upon which a story is flashed—the story of God. But behind this beautiful material reality there is another reality. It is an unseen reality that can be comprehended only by faith. It is tragic that man has become so blind that he cannot see the true spiritual story behind the physical facade (Job 12:7-9; 36:24-33; Psalms 8; 92:5,6; 94:8,9). Men say, "Why doesn't God show Himself?" The fact is, He does. It is not God's glory that prevents Him from being seen, but man's blindness. The Bible tells us that because God has revealed Himself so plainly in creation, men will be without excuse when they encounter His judgment (Romans 1:18-20). It is true that nature cannot reveal to men the way back to God. That is only done in His written revelation. But creation reveals that there is a God, that His power is infinitely beyond man's, and that He has certain claims upon the lives of His creatures.

Modern man looks at creation and says it proves evolution, when in reality it is an attestation to the power of Almighty God.

It could be that once men understood more from the creation than they do now. When Jesus was on earth, He turned frequently to natural illustrations: the lily, the sparrow, the harvest and the seed are only a few. Taking into consideration God's all-knowing foresight, it is clear that this was the reason these things were created in the first place. They were created to tell a story. Man's perception became so dim, however, that he largely lost the ability to see the true meaning of the material world. The written revelation of God was given to us to point us back to the reality of God, and especially to the clearest revelation of His glory—the incarnate Word, Jesus Christ. When John said, "In the beginning was the Word" (John 1:1), he was talking about the central idea behind all reality. A word is the crystallization of an idea, and the universe is the crystallization of God's Truth. When Jesus visited this planet, the light of God's glory shone at its zenith. He is the whole Idea.

John 1:14

GOD'S REVELATION IN THE WORD
(Psalm 19:7-14)

While verses 1-6 talk about God's revelation in the world, the rest of Psalm 19 talks about His revelation through His written Word.

We see that there are certain characteristics about God's Word that provide a benefit for us. There are six names given to the Word in this psalm: the law, the testimony, the statutes, the commandment, the fear, and the judgments. Each of these has a distinct emphasis and benefit. The "law" has to do with God's principles of conduct, and it is said to be perfect. It converts the soul. The literal meaning of "convert" here is *refresh*. Every believer knows how the Word refreshes his spiritual life! It is sure, and it makes the simple wise by giving them an accurate understanding of reality. The "statutes" of the Lord are His rules. Because they are right—straight and consistent—they make us happy and blessed when we observe them. The "commandments" of the Lord are said to be pure, or unmixed with any error. They help us to lead a clean, wholesome life.

The "fear" of the Lord is clean. The meaning of "clean" is *clear*. The Scriptures enable us to see clearly what God is like and what His will is for us. The "judgments" of the Lord are true and righteous. Because of this, they are more valuable than gold and sweeter than honey. One idea involved in His judgments is that they are His correct appraisal about things. When we have a clear view of the world it is most rewarding.

It is wonderful to know that we are not put into bondage by God's Word, but rather that He holds out to us explicit benefits for keeping it. The commandments of God are not given to us to make our lives harder, but to make them better. The shepherd's commands to his sheep are for the benefit of the sheep, not the shepherd. It is to keep them safe that he prods them with his rod or pulls them with his crook. Left to themselves, they might intrude upon forbidden mountains and be lost forever in the rough crags and rocks. His watchful gaze ever protects them from these dangers. And so it is with God. He leads us into the safest and best places.

In verses 12-14, David becomes concerned about the sins of the secret sanctuary, the heart.

The Word is just the right tonic to take when your spirit is drooping.

Wisdom has to do with looking at life with a God-ward view. The Word of God fits us with spiritual eyes that enable us to look at life through His eyes. See Ephesians 1:8 and Proverbs 2; 3.

See Psalm 19:11b.

See Deuteronomy 31:21; Psalm 44:21;

Romans 2:16.

An old poem by Hood tells about a killer who hid his victim in the river. Coming back the next day, he saw:

> *And sought the black accursed pool,*
> *With a wild misgiving eye;*
> *And he saw the dead in the river bed,*
> *And the faithless stream was dry.*

Then he covered the corpse with leaves, but the wind carried them away:

> *Then down I cast me on my face,*
> *And first began to weep,*
> *For I knew my secret then was one*
> *That earth refused to keep. . .*

Compare this with Genesis 4:9,10.

David likewise reminds us that there are no sins we can keep from God no matter where we hide them. We may try to bury all our old dead things, but they are always exposed to the Lord. Our errors are such that David exclaims: "Who can understand his errors?" The cleansing stream of God's Word is the agent to wash away the evil things in our hearts that even we are not fully aware of.

See John 15:3.

There are two things David is concerned about in this Psalm: the words of his mouth and the meditation of his heart. They are both open before the Lord. We have a tendency to think that our words just disappear, but the Bible reminds us that they are being recorded just as surely as one might record them on tape.

See James 3:2, where James says that the tongue is the key to self-control.

Being eyewitnesses to the first American president to resign, our generation has been made vividly aware of the power of recorded words.

29

The Watergate Tapes were the evidence that unseated an entire administration.

The Bible tells us that the evidence of our words will always be. Small wonder that David wanted his words to be acceptable in the sight of his Lord. One way for both our words and our thoughts to be acceptable in His sight is to build them around His Word. By building God's thoughts into our lives, our words and thoughts take on the likeness of God's thoughts.

Psalm 119:80 declares, "Let my heart be sound in thy statutes; that I be not ashamed."

It is surprising how much the Bible has to say about our spoken words. We are told that our words can be a net of flattery (Proverbs 2:16). They can be a snare to our lives (Proverbs 6:2). Words can destroy the poor (Isaiah 32:7). In fact, Jesus said that our words would be recorded and would come up against us on the day of judgment (Matthew 12:37).

It is a common thing to think that words merely evaporate like so much heated water. But that is not the picture we find in the Bible. We see there that words have a spiritual cause and effect. They are actually vehicles of spiritual energy.

Old Testament saints blessed and cursed their children with their words. Although God's way of doing things is not always the same, the principles remain. It is possible that we can also bless and curse with the tongue in a limited way (James 3:9). But God wants us to take seriously the words we say, and use our tongues to glorify Him.

Some positive ways to use our words for Him are to 1) pray; 2) witness wisely; 3) encourage others; 4) praise Him publicly; 5) teach; 6) preach; and 7) sing. The New Testament tells us to speak to ourselves in psalms and hymns (Ephesians 5:19), to exhort one another (Hebrews 10:25), and

We can become reflectors of God's glory by letting our tongues glorify Him. Through Christ we are partakers of that glory. We have seen the glory. As witnesses, we now tell others what we have seen.

to confess to one another (James 5:16). Although it is unwise to tell sordid details of past sins, we are commanded to confess to one another that we have need. This is a pathway to revival in the life of the Christian. To "confess" with our mouth means to say what God is saying. In its fullest sense, it means to line our words up with His Word.

The tongue is tiny, but untamed. Only by putting God's Word in our heart can we speak with the approval of God.

FOOD FOR THOUGHT

"A gossip is a person who will never tell a lie when the truth will do more damage."—The New Speaker's Sourcebook

NOW TEST YOUR KNOWLEDGE

Answer true or false:
1. All light comes from the heavenly bodies.
2. The heavenly bodies are reflectors of the glory of God.
3. Nature shows us how to be saved.
4. Natural creation was given to us to reveal the God behind that creation, but man's sin hid the message.
5. In Psalm 19, God's Word is called by six names: the law, the testimony, the statutes, the commandments, the fear and the judgments.
6. God's rules are right in certain situations.
7. God gave us His Word, not to put us into bondage, but to benefit us.

It is only in the secret sanctuary of the heart that we can hide our sins from God.

poken words have a spiritual significance today they did in the Old Testament.

'confess" means to say the same thing God is

?.

31

I Am Redeemed

LESSON SCRIPTURE
Psalms 22; 16; 72

RELATED SCRIPTURE
Psalms 2; 23; 24; 41; 69; 110

LESSON AIM
To increase confidence in the Scriptures
as the inspired Word of God.

LEARN BY HEART
"Thou wilt shew me the path of life: in thy
presence is fulness of joy; at thy right hand
there are pleasures for evermore (Psalm
16:11).

4

EVERY DAY WITH THE WORD

Monday	"Thou art my Son"	Psalm 2
Tuesday	"Thou art holy"	Psalm 22
Wednesday	"He restoreth my soul"	Psalm 23
Thursday	"Blessed be the Lord God"	Psalm 41
Friday	"I wait for my God"	Psalm 69
Saturday	"The Lord. . . will not repent"	Psalm 110
Sunday	"The King of glory"	Psalm 24

STUDENT'S NOTEBOOK

This column is fo
student who des
additional study
the lesson ther

LESSON PREPARATION

The popular magazines give us predictions of
the seers almost weekly. Their predictions about
popular entertainers and well-known politicians
are brought before us for our observation and
entertainment. Daily, in 1,200 newspapers, the
horoscope section is read eagerly by a gullible

public trying to plot the destinies of their lives. In our neighborhood streets, palm readers and other fortune tellers beckon people to their dark rooms. Strangely, the predictions the prophets miss are not heard of. But when one ''hits'' an event, it is ballyhooed as a marvelous bit of business.

In the Old Testament, God was also having some dealings with the seers and false prophets. He told the children of Israel how they could tell a true prophet from a prophet of God. If a prophet predicted a thing and it did not come to pass *every time,* he was simply not a true prophet. God's prophets hit the nail on the head every time. The power of Satan, or even chance, could enable a prophet to predict an event sometimes. But when the Spirit of God is speaking, He can speak only the truth.

This is extremely relevant today when we consider "seers" who have claimed they are prophets of God. But God reminds us that if a prophet fails in his prophecy, he is not the Lord's prophet (Deuteronomy 18:22).

THE REDEEMER REJECTED
(Psalm 22)

With all the trouble in the world, the world is looking for a man who can relieve the suffering and lead us to a higher plateau. If only somebody would come along who could heal the sick, raise the dead, give us wisdom about how to live our lives and show us a better way to live, we would let him lead us to a better day. Right? Wrong. That is exactly what did happen once, but instead of turning things over to Him, we rejected His claim to leadership and killed Him as a common criminal on a Roman cross. His name was Jesus Christ. And that rejection and crucifixion was prophesied, a thousand years before it happened, in the Twenty-Second Psalm.

If Jesus were to appear suddenly at the United Nations He would likely be shut out. The world has had 2,000 years to examine His record, but most of the world still does not believe.

The rejection and crucifixion of Christ were

both in the plan of God. And while the events served to contrast the righteousness of Christ against the blackness of man's heart, it was the only way that corrupted man could be redeemed. At one moment occurred the darkest and brightest spot in human history: darkest because it underscored the awful potential of the sinful hearts of fallen men; brightest because it was the pivotal point to turn man to God.

From the very beginning in the garden of Eden (Genesis 3:15), on through the Old Testament prophets, God had foretold the death of the Redeemer. Two of the sharpest instances of these prophecies are Isaiah, chapter 53, and the Twenty-Second Psalm.

Psalm 22 opens with the cry of our Saviour, "My God, my God, why hast thou forsaken me?" Repeated word for word as Jesus hung on the cross, these words are just one more indication of the accuracy of the Scriptures. It is inconceivable that the two could match so clearly aside from fulfilled prophecy. History and the textual evidence for the Old Testament confirm that one is the literal fulfillment of the other.

This utterance also demonstrates the awful suffering that Jesus endured on the cross. He died for us. The Bible meaning of *death* involves *separation*. In some way that is beyond our understanding, the Father turned His back on the Son as the Son became sin for us. We can realize partially the extent of this amazing happening by thinking of our own sin. If we could recall the most shameful, despicable thing that we have ever done, we can realize what it might have been like for the Saviour to *become* that for us. Then, when that is multiplied by the sum total of all man's sin, it is no

The Bible shows that saving faith must have as its object the death of Christ on the cross. See Romans 3:25.

wonder that the Saviour shrank from that cup in the garden. And it is clear to see why a holy God would turn from the thing that His Son was identifying with in His awful death. It was not merely individual acts of sin, but the sin principle itself that He took upon Himself. It was the whole corrupting, terrible spectacle of man's depraved nature.

When we see the horror of the sin question as it is pictured in the cross, it is small wonder that God hates it. And we can see what we would have to endure if we were not redeemed by His blood.

Other details of the death of Christ depicted in the Twenty-Second Psalm are His reproach: ''But I am a worm, and no man'' (verse 6); the mockery of the people (verses 6-8,12,13); the uniqueness of His birth (verses 9,10); the intense suffering (verses 14,15); crucifixion as the manner of execution (verse 16); His being stripped (verse 17); the casting of lots for His garments (verse 18).

For a full range of Messianic prophecies see Halley's Bible Handbook, pages 387-401.

It is cause enough for wonder when we view the historical scene itself. But when we see God's painting of that climactic day recorded a thousand years ahead of time by the pen of the prophet David, we may well marvel at the accuracy of Scripture.

At the time this was written, the accepted form of execution among the Jews was stoning. Crucifixion was an innovation of the Romans many years later.

THE REDEEMER RETURNING
(Psalms 16; 72)

The words of General Douglas MacArthur have become a permanent part of the American heritage. When he was forced to leave the Philippine Islands during the Second World War, he uttered his determined promise, ''I shall return!'' He did

35

return, and history records the end of the story.

The Lord Jesus Christ also made the promise, "I shall return." Before He died on the cross, He said that He would return after three days, just as Jonah had returned from the belly of the whale. The prophecy in Psalms concerning this is found in Psalm 16:8-10.

David was probably speaking primarily of his hope of resurrection. But the prophetic Scriptures go beyond the immediate setting to picture coming events. We see that prophetically, this passage has to do with the unusual circumstances surrounding the death of the Lord Jesus Christ. God would have us know that Jesus died on the cross, having a body like ours. Also, He would have us know that Jesus arose from the dead. You will remember how the New Testament tells us that Joseph and Nicodemus took the body down and buried it in a new tomb, hewn in a hillside. The body was dead. The warmth of life was gone. The death of Jesus was not an illusion, but an actual occurrence.

You will remember that at the raising of Lazarus, Martha said that because he had been dead four days, decaying would have set in and there would be the odor of death when the tomb was opened. That is why we bury bodies. We want to get the sight and the smell of death out of our presence. It is part of the curse of sin. But there was something different about the death of Christ; something that set it apart from every other death that ever occurred. In the three days that the body of Jesus lay in the grave, no decaying took place. This remarkable fact is spelled out in Psalm 16:10: "For thou wilt not leave my soul in hell [Sheol]; neither wilt thou suffer thine Holy One to

Although we must believe in the death of Christ for our sins, we also must have faith in a living Saviour. Had He stayed dead our faith would be vain.

36

Sometimes the Bible uses the word "corruption" to describe the whole process of sin and its result. Corrupting carcasses are a constant reminder of the terrible consequences of sin. See I Corinthians 15:42-50,53.

John 14:3; Acts 1:11

In Revelation 20:1 seven years of severe judgment upon the earth (Matthew 24).

see corruption." Corruption describes the process of decay. Although the Saviour took our place on the cross, because He was holy His body could see no corruption. The New Testament describes how that holy body arose, changed into a new dimension and glory.

Not only were the birth and life of the Lord Jesus Christ different from all others, but His death was different as well. Christ was not just another man that crossed the stage of the world's history. He was God the Son.

Both before and after His death and resurrection, Jesus promised that He would return. God had already given messianic hope in the Law of Moses, enlarged it in the Psalms and poetic Scriptures, and made it shine in full brightness in the prophets. Then after Christ's resurrection the disciples understood that the risen Lord was the Messiah of the Old Testament Scriptures, and that He would return to establish His righteous kingdom.

In Psalm 72 we see some references to the coming King. The first few verses show us that His reign will be equitable and just. Peace will be the condition on earth for a thousand years. Although poverty will not be eliminated, the poor will be cared for. We can be sure that the righteous King will let nobody starve (see Psalm 72:4).

Verse 7 tells us that the merit system during that time will revolve around righteous behavior. In verses 8-11 we learn that the reigning Lord will exercise absolute authority. No abusive or lawless activity will be tolerated.

Verses 15,16 tell of the riches and fruitfulness of the time when Jesus will reign from Jerusalem on the throne of His father David. Other prophetic passages specify how the curse will be lifted.

Thorns and thistles, the sign of the curse, will no longer infest the ground, and wild and domestic animals will lie down together. It will be a time of glorious prosperity and blessing.

Genesis 3:18; Isaiah 55:13

We are reminded in verse 17 that men will be blessing His name rather than taking it in vain, as many do now. The name on every tongue and the subject of conversation will be the One who was once despised and rejected. The house of God will be exalted, violence will be done away with, and righteousness will be the rule rather than the exception.

In the model prayer Jesus taught His disciples to pray, ''Thy kingdom come. Thy will be done in earth, as it is in heaven'' (Matthew 6:10). Our hearts should long for the time when the Saviour will bring peace and justice to this ravaged earth.

Think of how awkward it is now to sit down with a group and start talking about Jesus. But during the kingdom, His name will be discussed everywhere. He is now in the place of rejection in this world. But then, He will be the reigning Monarch.

FOOD FOR THOUGHT

Because He cried, "My God, my God, why hast thou forsaken me?" we don't have to.

Answer true or false:

1. A prophet is true if everything he prophesies comes to pass.
2. If only someone could come along to relieve the world's suffering, everyone would crown him king.
3. God began telling of the death of the Redeemer at the very beginning of His Word.
4. At the cross we see nothing of God's hatred for sin, but only His love for us.
5. Psalm 22 foretold the crucifixion in graphic detail.
6. The word "corruption" describes the awful result of sin.
7. The death of Jesus was just like every other death in that His body began to decay.
8. Only the spirit of Jesus arose from the dead.
9. The Scriptures teach that Jesus Christ will rule on earth for a thousand years.
10. In order to give men more of a chance to be saved, we are not to pray for the coming of Christ's kingdom.

A Thirst for God

LESSON SCRIPTURE
Psalms 42; 43

RELATED SCRIPTURE
Psalms 63; 64; II Samuel 17; John 4:1-39;
7:37-39

LESSON AIM
To realize the satisfaction which is found
in God.

LEARN BY HEART
"As the hart panteth after the water
brooks, so panteth my soul after thee, O
God" (Psalm 42:1).

EVERY DAY WITH THE WORD

Monday	Defense	Psalm 62
Tuesday	Satisfaction	Psalm 63
Wednesday	Preservation	Psalm 64
Thursday	Health	Psalm 42
Friday	Guidance	Psalm 43
Saturday	Life	John 4:1-23
Sunday	Deliverance	John 4:24-39

STUDENT'S NOTEBOOK

This column is for the student who desires additional study of the lesson theme.

LESSON PREPARATION

Bob Smith treaded water for more than a day in the Ten Thousand Islands that lie between the waters of the Gulf of Mexico and the marshy coast of the Florida Everglades. His tiny fishing boat had capsized and gone under, leaving him in the darkness. All through the night, the next day and into the dusk of another night, the big, burly man kept himself afloat in the salty waters of the Gulf. It was a remarkable display of strength.

The hardest thing Smith had to endure was the thirst. The Florida sun bore down upon him, drawing perspiration freely. His throat became dry, although he was surrounded by water. He often wondered if thirst would be the thing that would finally cause his strength to fail. He could not drink the water he was floating in for it would only have made his thirst worse. It was sea water, unfit for human consumption. Only the fresh, cool water of a well would avail. When a fisherman finally pulled Smith out of the water, the first thing he wanted was a drink of water.

Like Smith in the sea, the masses of mankind are thrashing about just to survive. There is nothing around them that can satisfy their thirst. They desperately need the "water of life" in order to experience true, lasting, spiritual satisfaction.

In Psalm 42, David finds himself in exile because of the rebellion of his son, Absalom. He remembers his former state and wants the fellowship of God and His people.

THE EXILE REMEMBERING GOD
(Psalm 42)

As David remembers God, he expresses his feelings in verse 1. As a deer in the dry season in the Middle East would thirst for the brook where the fresh water flowed, David thirsted for the living God. This brings to mind one of the Beatitudes: "Blessed are they which do hunger and thirst after righteousness: for they shall be filled" (Matthew 5:6). The Scriptures remind us

Thirst can be spiritual as well as physical. The spiritual, or heart, longing often drives a person to satisfy that thirst through drugs, alcohol or some other means.

Ultimately, this hunger and thirst for righteousness can

that it is better to thirst for spiritual satisfaction in righteousness than to thirst for the water of this world. Thirst for water is a picture of the emptiness of a soul without God. Just as God created the physical body with a thirst for water, even so He created the soul of man with a thirst for Himself.

In his time of great need, David expresses the thought in Psalm 42:2 that only source of true satisfaction is the living God. A less perceptive person might be tempted to think that deliverance from the present circumstances would bring satisfaction. But, spiritually speaking, that would be the same thing as if Bob Smith had drunk of the salt water. It would only create more thirst. The outer circumstances of life cannot satisfy the deep longings of our souls. Only God can do that. So David cried out, "My soul thirsteth for God, for the living God" (Psalm 42:2).

Never mind the circumstances. It was not his throne or his comfortable royal surroundings that David thirsted for. Only God would satisfy. This is a lesson for us in our testings. It is not God's getting us out of trouble that is important, it is *God* who is the solution. Hebrews 11:6 tells us that He is a rewarder of those who seek *Him,* not His gifts or His help. Once having gained Him, we have everything.

Those around David did not understand his situation. A person without strong faith will always look at the nature of the circumstances. In his exile and trouble, David said in verse 3, his tormentors were continually asking, "Where is thy God?" This reminds us of the accusations hurled at Christ while He was on the cross. "He trusted in God; let him deliver him" (Matthew 27:43). Likewise the friends of Job reasoned that

be met only by Christ. See John 6:57,63; 7:37.

Many people think it is impossible to be satisfied if physical circumstances are unfavorable. But note Paul's content in spite of some of the worst trials man can go through (Philippians 4:6-13).

since Job was suffering, he must surely be a terrible sinner. One of the most difficult things to do is to maintain a stedfast faith in God despite appearances.

Matthew 20:1-15

In the parable of the field workers, Jesus told about workers who complained of the husbandman's generosity to the latecomers. The idea was that he owed the early comers a special consideration, too. We somehow get the idea that God is obligated to give us complete happiness and prosperity. And when He doesn't appear to we become bitter toward Him. We either think it doesn't pay to serve Him, or that He loves others more than us. Added to this, there are the taunts of our accusers. They are always there to remind us that we were wrong all along to trust in an invisible God. Their attitude is, "Look at what's happening. If it pays to serve God, why is this happening to you?" Perhaps that is why David sensed the need for a special closeness to God—to demonstrate to his own soul that God was still there.

For another instance where a person talks to his soul, see Luke 12:19.

With these thoughts in mind, David begins to assure his own soul. He has a conversation with his innermost being. First, in Psalm 42:4, he remembers that there was a time when he worshiped with the multitude, leading them to the house of God. David had the spiritual awareness to realize that mental depression was not the same as spiritual defeat. Four times, in verses 5,6,11 and 43:5, David notes that his soul is "cast down." Our spirits are sure to react to adverse circumstances, but God remains the same in spite of our reaction. In his prayer in Psalm 42:6, David shares with God that his soul is cast down, even after expressing hope in verse 3 that it would only be a temporary condition. The remedy for this depression is simple: "Therefore will I remember thee" (verse 6).

In verse 7 David's problems remind him of the waterspouts which he had no doubt often seen. Many are the times when we, too, are overwhelmed by our troubles. David's answer is to tell God all about it. He even rehearses his prayer ahead of time. After he reminds us in verse 8 that God's lovingkindness will overcome his deep troubles, and that He will give him songs in the night, David says, "I will say unto God my rock, Why hast thou forgotten me?" That is the way David's soul felt, and he would share it with the living God. It is a mistake to feel that we should not pray unless we "feel" like it.

Verses 10 and 11 repeat the themes of verses 3 and 5, characteristic of the form of poetry employed in these sacred writings. The repetition was for emphasis. Another thought David repeated often in these verses is that God was the help of his countenance. It is a fact that the light of our countenance reflects the inward condition of the soul. David was merely observing that when things are right with God on the inside, there will be an eventual indication of it on the outside.

THE EXILE RETURNING TO GOD'S HOUSE (Psalm 43)

Most observers feel that Psalms 42 and 43 were originally together as one, for the thoughts of Psalm 42 continue in Psalm 43. In Psalm 43 David seems to gain assurance that he will be returning to the house of God. It is significant that David associates the reality of God with the house of

"Waterspouts" in the King James Version has the meaning of channels or gutters for water to run off a building. In Psalm 42 it is a reference to the waters running off the land in violent torrents and cataracts (waterfalls).

Is our time with God in prayer important enough for us to give careful thought and preparation to it ahead of time?

Note what the Bible says about the change in the countenance of the Lord Jesus Christ at the transfiguration in Luke 9:29. Compare that with the countenance of the hypocrites in Matthew 6:16.

The following are
important
observations about
the "assembly," or
"church." It involves
a group of people, a
stated meeting
place, an
organizational
structure and a
means of identifying
who the believers
are.

See Hebrews
10:24,25.

God. It was God Himself who appointed a definite place for the children of Israel to assemble and worship, just as He appointed the church, or assembly, in the New Testament.

In exile in the wilderness, David was exposed to all the taunts and unbelief of his enemies. We are in the same position when we go out into the world. This present world is a stranger to grace. It is only when we can worship and share with our own kind that we have a complete worship experience. To be sure, the presence of God goes with us everywhere. But God has ordained that unity of spirit with others, congregational praise, oneness of purpose and compatibility of belief all blend together to make up the worship of the saints. The believer who absents himself from the assembly of believers is only robbing himself of a reality and expression of worship that cannot be experienced any other way.

In Psalm 43:1 David asks God to discern between his cause and that of his enemies. It is a safe course for a righteous man to pray in that manner. Because he is confident of the rightness of his cause, David pleads for deliverance in the latter part of the verse. A clear conscience is a strong weapon in our arsenal.

In verse 2, David asks that if God is his strength, why is he in the present distress because of his enemies? Again, the righteous heart can dare to ask "why?" David is not asking out of unbelief, but out of confidence that God would provide the answer.

Bill and Jim were both experiencing great difficulty in their lives. Bill kept saying, "I just can't understand why all this is happening to me." He didn't search his Bible for the answer. He didn't

45

use the occasion to increase his prayer life. Bill never did find the answer. He just kept getting more bitter. Jim, on the other hand, said, "I don't really understand all about what I am going through in my life right now. But I have set aside extra times for Bible study and prayer until God gives me the answers." It is not difficult to figure out which of the two was praying in the same spirit in which David prayed.

In Psalm 43:2 David is praying for light and leadership. It was not for his own interests, but that he might be led back to the house of God. In verse 5, David makes a promise to God that when he returns to the house of God he will praise Him, probably upon the harp.

In verse 5, David once again converses with his own soul and expresses hope. Hope is the beacon that shines through the darkness of the present circumstances to the brightness of the coming deliverance. There is only one place in which our hope can safely trust: "Hope in God," David tells his soul. This is good advice for all of us as well.

Judging from the fact that David was called to the court of King Saul early in his life to play the harp in the king's court, his harp playing must have been skillful and in great demand. Add to this the fact that he was the king, and we can picture the huge audience David would have for his concert of praise!

FOOD FOR THOUGHT

"Thou, Lord, bruisest me, but I am abundantly satisfied, since it is from thy hand."
                                        –John Calvin

Answer true or false:

1. Our thirst for physical water is a picture of our deeper spiritual thirst for God.
2. Trying to satisfy our spiritual thirst by the things of this world only creates more thirst.
3. When a person is having outward difficulty, it always reveals that he is not right with God.
4. It is not possible to talk with your own soul.
5. It is sometimes advisable to rehearse ahead of time what you will be praying about.
6. A person's countenance has nothing to do with his soul.
7. It doesn't matter to God where a person worships, as long as he worships.
8. It is right to ask God to judge between a righteous person and his enemies.
9. When we are experiencing difficulty, it is not necessary to set aside extra times for Bible study and prayer.
10. Hope does not do a person any good when he is in dark circumstances.

He Lifted Me!

LESSON SCRIPTURE
Psalm 40

RELATED SCRIPTURE
Psalms 18; 70

LESSON AIM
To express appreciation for God's deliverance by grace.

LEARN BY HEART
"And he hath put a new song in my mouth, even praise unto our God: many shall see it, and fear, and shall trust in the Lord" (Psalm 40:3).

EVERY DAY WITH THE WORD

Monday	God's power	Psalm 18:1-15
Tuesday	God's provision	Psalm 18:16-34
Wednesday	God's protection	Psalm 18:35-50
Thursday	God's promises	II Corinthians 1
Friday	God's preservation	I Peter 1:1-12
Saturday	God's redemption	I Peter 1:13-25
Sunday	God's response	Psalm 40

STUDENT'S NOTEBOOK

This column is for the student who desires additional study of the lesson theme.

LESSON PREPARATION

Fifty years ago old pit wells provided cool, refreshing water for rural farms. Occasionally, one of the wells would go dry. And on rare occasions a child would fall into a half-hidden, unkept well. This was a time of horror for the parents who waited while crews worked to dig a rescue shaft beside the one where the child was. Workers

The prophet Jeremiah was imprisoned in a pit (Jeremiah 37; 38).

"Pit" is usually a reference to a water cistern dug out of the earth and lined with lime plaster to make it waterproof. The access to the cistern was usually a hole just about wide enough for a man to drop down through it.

Stone to cover hole—to keep animals out or prisoners in

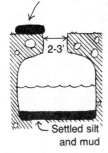

2-3'

Settled silt and mud

See Genesis 37:24.

The difference between "waiting" and being slothful can be explained by the fact that a person can wait on God while being both physically and mentally active. "Waiting" signifies

could often hear the drip, drip of water seeping in and an occasional falling of soil and rock.

There is something ominous about looking down into a pit. It is dark, foreboding and uncertain. In Bible days, pits were used for prisons. Attempts to climb up were useless. There were no windows or doors through which to escape. The bottom was slippery, sticky and filthy. Water ran in through crevices. Darkness added to the confinement of already close quarters, spelling the utmost in discomfort. The pit became a fitting symbol of the condition of the sinner, and was often used as a synonym for Hell.

In praising God for deliverance, the psalmist pictures himself in Psalm 40 as crying from the pit, then being lifted up and put upon the solid rock.

PRAISE FOR PAST DELIVERANCE
(Psalm 40:1-10)

"I waited patiently for the Lord," David begins in this song of praise (Psalm 40:1). "Waiting" and "patience" are two words that speak of faith. Waiting implies that the psalmist did not take matters into his own hands and work out his own way to be delivered. And not only did he wait, but he also waited with patience. He had the attitude that no matter how difficult or how long the wait, God would deliver him. There are matters that require our own strength, but divine deliverance is not one of them.

Soon David's patience paid off. God heard David's cry when He inclined unto him. The word "inclined" contains the idea of bowing down. It

49

is a fitting picture of the grace of God. The sinner is in the pit, crying out, and God bows down to meet his need. The Lord Jesus bowed all the way down until He met us at the bottom of the pit.

an attitude, not a state of inactivity.

See Philippians 2:5-9.

The pit is described in verse 2 as "horrible." One scholar has suggested that this refers to noise, the kind made by dripping water. The clay is called "miry." We are reminded that there are a thousand miry places to catch the sinner's feet. Taken together, these two descriptions are fitting in their portrayal of the condition of the unredeemed sinner.

The Lord did three things to meet the need of the waiting sinner, as explained in verse 2. He not only inclined and heard, but David says He also "brought me up"; He "set my feet upon a rock"; He "established my goings." The sinner does not climb up out of the pit himself, for he cannot. He has to be brought up. Since the pit is a picture of our lost condition, it is clear to see that we cannot save ourselves. He must bring us up. Salvation is of the Lord. After bringing us out, God sets us upon the Rock, Jesus Christ. He is the only foundation (I Corinthians 3:11). Then He establishes our goings by giving us direction and purpose, and a permanent place in His eternal plan.

The result of God's work in a life is that the delivered one has a song to sing. There are many references in the Psalms to "a new song," probably because these poems were originally written to be set to music. But "a new song" is also associated with redemption (see Revelation 5:9). It is not until the erring sinner experiences redemption that he has this new song. Surely, our redemption gives us a song that we could never

Music has always held an important place in worship, in both the Old and New Testaments (See I Chronicles 6:31; Colossians 3:16). Music will also have a prominent place in Heaven (see

Revelation 5:9; 14:3; 15:3).

sing before, a song of praise for His matchless grace. Because of the new joy of heart, Psalm 40:3 says, "Many shall see it, and fear, and shall trust in the Lord." Our new song is so different from the minor key in which the world sings that it points people to our Redeemer.

This is a contradiction to one of the favorite messages of Satan. He would have the world believe that if one becomes a believer, all his joy will be gone. The reverse, of course, is true. And it is the particular privilege of the redeemed sinner to show the world the new song that comes from being delivered by grace.

Ruth, a young mother, is a dynamic, growing Christian. She has her troubles at times, like anyone. But Ruth feels that it is a ministry to portray a happy and pleasant disposition.

"When I smile sometimes," she said, "it is not for me. There are times when I really don't feel like smiling. But a smile is a help to others."

Shirley, on the other hand, has the foolish idea that it is hypocritical to smile if you don't feel like it. Shirley has forgotten that dampened spirits do not mean an end to joy. We have an obligation to display our Christian joy.

Joy does not arise from favorable circumstances. It is part of the fruit of the Spirit (Galatians 5:22).

We are introduced to the blessed man again in Psalm 40:4. He is the man who trusts in the Lord. And surely the one who places his confidence in the Lord will receive limitless blessings.

Verse 5 reminds us that God's thoughts and works toward us are more than we can possibly calculate.

In verses 6-8 we see that David was willing to do the Father's will even if it meant partaking of death. These verses are quoted by the Messiah, according to the author of Hebrews, as He de-

51

scribes His unspeakable sacrifice (Hebrews 10:5-7). We are reminded that since the Saviour said, "Not my will, but thine, be done," in the dark garden of His trial (Luke 22:42), we should be willing to say the same thing when our circumstances are dark.

Sam is saved, but you wouldn't know it. He has never breathed a word of testimony to his friends. The people at work have never heard him say anything about the Lord, and he has not even said anything to the members of his family. David, the king of Israel, was not like that. In Psalm 40:9,10, he says that he will not hide the truth of God in his own heart. "I have not hid thy righteousness within my heart," he declares. "I have not concealed thy lovingkindness and thy truth."

If we were to find a priceless gem, it would be hard to conceal our excitement from others. And it ought to be so with our redemption. Salvation is such a marvelous possession that we should not shun to declare it to others. It is easy enough to remain silent. But the God whose grace lifted us out of the pit is sufficient to give us the courage to witness. David says, "I have preached" (verse 9) and "I have declared" (verse 10).

We need to remember that David did not fit the mold that we would imagine now for a "full-time Christian worker." He was the king. His witnessing had to be done in the midst of his other duties. But that did not excuse him from declaring to others the deliverance that he had experienced.

Even in the days of the early church, the ideas of "sacred" versus "secular" and "clergy" versus "laity" had not evolved to the state in which we find them today. Contrary to common belief, it is the consistent inference of Scripture that *every*

Although the pulpit offers opportunity and advantages that are unique, and has an important place in the proclamation of the gospel, one does not have to stand in a pulpit to preach. The word "preach" means "to bring good tidings." We can all do that.

believer has the obligation to be a witness for his Redeemer.

PRAYER FOR FUTURE DEFENSE
(Psalm 40:11-17)

Having given praise for past deliverance, David goes on to plead for God to grant him continued protection and deliverance in the future. This is a sound idea. Because God has exercised such a great deliverance in our behalf in the past, we can look to the future with faith. We start with our deliverance from sin and go on from there. Peter, in his second epistle, points out some things that we should add to our faith, such as virtue, patience, and so on (II Peter 1:5-7). Failing to do this, he adds, results in a lack of vision for the future. "But he that lacketh these things is blind, and cannot see afar off, and hath forgotten that he was purged from his old sins" (II Peter 1:9). We dare not forget the great deliverance that God has provided by His grace.

In Psalm 40:11-13, one of the things that David is acutely aware of is his need for continuing mercy. The believer does not merely receive mercy in his initial deliverance and then operate on his own after that. He needs God's mercy throughout his pilgrim journey (Hebrews 4:16). David is keenly aware of his sins and iniquities. In Psalm 40:12, he says that his iniquities have such power over him that they have become innumerable, "more than the hairs of mine head." He was so overwhelmed by his own spiritual infirmity that he could say, "my heart faileth me." There is reason to suspect that many of us are suffering

Paul admonishes us to present our bodies to God, based upon recalling the "mercies of God" (Romans 12:1,2).

In contrast, Jesus said that the hairs of our head are all numbered.

from spiritual heart failure. What is the remedy?

Psalm 40 reveals that the remedy for spiritual heart failure is to learn that the grace and kindness of God is more than a match for our infirmity. Although David's iniquities seemed without number, he had also discovered that God's provision is without calculation: "If I would declare and speak of them, they are more than can be numbered" (verse 5).

Sin causes hardening of the hearteries, but God's grace is a most effective cure.

We are told that a modern computer can, in seconds, solve problems that would take a mathematician more than a thousand years to solve. One computer analyst has said that a computer can solve in thirty seconds a problem that Adam would still be working on! This expert concluded by saying laughingly that "the only things a computer can't solve are the things that don't add up." Psalm 40:5 speaks of one of those things. So staggering are the works of God in our behalf that even one of these electronic marvels could not count them.

How wonderful to know that no matter how overwhelming our infirmities, they are more than matched by the mighty grace of God!

In verses 14,15 another problem confronts the writer. His own infirmities have given occasion for his enemies to accuse him. It is bad enough that people talk about us. But when their accusations contain an element of truth, the adversary accuses our consciences all the more. The picture here is of those who have been waiting in the wings to catch David in a fault, just as wicked men tried to catch his divine Descendant in a fault many centuries later. The enemies' reaction to David's stumbling is found in verse 15: "Let them be desolate for a reward of their shame that say

The answer to pangs of conscience is not to suppress, but to confess (see I John 1:9).

Although none could accuse Jesus, David could be accused because he was a mere man.

years behind the current market, because he didn't believe in financing cars. Besides, he argued, "Why should a fellow take such a beating on a new car as soon as he drives it off the showroom floor?"

Stu always prayed for his brother, Carl, a bright, outgoing man who had not yet been saved. But Stu was having some problems along that line, for Carl was a gifted man who seemed to succeed at everything he did. His home was about twice as large as Stewart's, and he always drove a new car. Whenever Stu and his family would visit Carl's home, the children enjoyed swimming in the pool, and Stu's wife always expressed disappointment that they did not have nice things like Carl's family had. And Stu had to admit that he would like to be as well off as his brother was. It wasn't fair that an unsaved man could have so much, Stu argued.

Then one night at a special church service, the evangelist preached a message on Hell that really stirred the whole Mills family. When they had their family altar each evening the following week, the children broke down and cried for their aunt, uncle and cousins. Stu's wife was especially broken in her concern for them. A few months later, the Lord began to convict Carl and he soon came to know the Lord. Other members of his family were also reached for Christ. The Mills were glad that their envy had turned to a genuine concern.

Webster's Dictionary defines "envy" as "a feeling of discontent and ill will because of another's advantages." Hatred and unhappiness are wrapped up in the word "envy." It is impossible to envy someone and love him at the same time.

CONFIDENCE IN GOD'S PROMISES
(Psalm 37:1-20)

The Mills were making the mistake that many

Christians make. They were looking at the outward circumstances of others and thinking that worldly prosperity was the same thing as well-being. They had taken their eyes off the promises of God that spoke of better things than good circumstances. But when the Lord spoke to them about the reality of Hell, they were thankful that they had been delivered from its terror. And they began to see that their relatives were not so well off, after all.

Read I John 2:15-17. Better still, memorize I John 2:15-17.

In Psalm 37, God warns us of the folly of envying the wicked. In doing so, He reminds us of both the blessings of the just and the end of the unjust. In this Psalm we are warned three times not to do something that many Christians today practice. We are to avoid "fretting" (verses 1,7,8), which means to "be angry."

In verse 8 God says, "Fret not thyself in any wise to do evil." The Bible warns us that when we envy the wicked we become emotionally tied to them in such a way that we are in danger of becoming like them. There is a secret thing that happens in our hearts almost without our knowing it. We start getting the idea that it pays to be like them. Instead of being thankful for the Lord's blessings, we secretly become dissatisfied with our lot and wish things were different. Looking about us, we see the apparent prosperity of the unsaved and imagine that it would be better to be like them. It is not hard to see how that kind of thinking can soon bring us into spiritual bondage. We become like those we are envying.

We cannot be free of someone we envy or hate. Our envy creates an emotional tie that is a constant reminder of our discomfort (see Esther 5:13).

In this song of instruction, God gives us some precious and liberating promises that can counteract that kind of fallacious thinking. There are four exhortations, coupled with accompanying promises, that are given to us for our good.

The first exhortation is to "trust" (verse 3). This means to have confidence that, no matter what appearances convey, it is better to put confidence in the Lord than in men. An old, but true, saying advises, "Never judge a well by the length of the pump handle." It is unwise to trust in appearances. But it is wise to trust in the Lord. Verse 4 continues, "Trust in the Lord and do good." The thought is to trust God that if we do good as He commands, He will reward us. The reward is clearly set forth: "So shalt thou dwell in the land, and verily thou shalt be fed." We will not want for temporal provision. And beyond meeting our physical needs, He feeds us with the living Bread and shelters us with the tabernacle of His presence. That is worth more than all the material wealth the world has to offer.

The second exhortation is, "Delight thyself also in the Lord" (verse 4). It is still true, as our Lord told us, that our treasure is where our heart is (Matthew 6:21). Therefore if we delight ourselves in the Lord, we will treasure His presence, His service, His worship, and His blessings. When we secretly envy the wicked, their treasures become our coveted treasures.

Scripture gives us abundant promises that we will be blessed if we make the Lord the delight of our hearts. "Thou shalt love the Lord thy God with all thy heart," is the first and great commandment (Matthew 22:37,38). The promise given to us in Psalm 37:4 shows that when we have such love for Him, we can expect to receive the desires of our hearts. Our hearts are deceptive and wicked, so we cannot really know the true desires of our own hearts (Jeremiah 17:9). But

When Satan appeared to Eve in the garden, he was beautiful but treacherous. So often the things of the world are like this.

God can show us what our desires are and then grant them to us. If most believers would just stop to think, they would not trade the peace of forgiveness for all the material riches in the world. They would not trade the wisdom and guidance of God's Word for money, status, or power.

The third exhortation is found in verse 5: "Commit thy way unto the Lord." To "commit" speaks of charting our course in a certain direction. "Way" speaks of a path or road. God is simply telling us to chart our course along His pathways. The promise that accompanies this command is decisive: "And he will bring it to pass." Anything that is godly and blessed can fit under the heading of "it." When we get down to the end of life's road, we will find that everything we could have desired was brought to pass by Him. The wicked, on the other hand, will find that their road leads to disaster. One day everyone will know that it was the righteous man who was right (verse 6).

The Bible lights our way along God's path (see Psalm 119:105).

Read again Psalm 1.

The fourth command is found in verse 7, which tells us to "rest in the Lord." Resting is the opposite of fretting. Those who envy are always pining away because they are dissatisfied with their lot in life, but those who are resting in the Lord are content with what they have.

See Hebrews 4:9-11; 13:5,6.

In the midst of many other verses that warn us of the end of the wicked, we are promised in verse 11 that we will finally inherit the whole earth if we wait on Him to accomplish His will. The meek "shall inherit the earth," we are told in Matthew 5:5.

It is sad that those who reject the promises of God will one day find that their meager temporal possessions cannot give lasting satisfaction. For those things will be taken because the heavens and the earth will belong to the people of God. We are promised in the book of Revelation that we will reign with the Lord Jesus for a thousand years here on this earth and then throughout eternity we will share, as joint heirs with Him, the whole universe. When we trust Him, we can wait and rest in His promises.

CONFIDENCE IN GOD'S PROVISION
(Psalm 37:21-40)

God wants us to learn a lesson of quality: the kind of blessing we receive is more important than the quantity of material things we possess. Certain intangible provisions are far superior to those possessions that are more visible. For example, there is the blessing of having a liberal heart, as opposed to being stingy. In Psalm 37:21 the psalmist contrasts the good man and the wicked man by saying that the wicked man is always seeking to get, whereas the good man seeks to give. A grasping heart is a terrible condition to have. Even though a man in such a condition may accumulate more for awhile, he never really enjoys his gain because he is always wanting more.

Direction is another provision that the Lord has for the just, as verse 23 says. The steps of a righteous man are ordered by the Lord. There are times that he will stumble, but he cannot fall, for he is held up by the almighty hand of his Saviour.

To liberality and direction we can add security. Verse 25 tells us that God has never forsaken His righteous children. And according to Hebrews 13:5,6, He never will.

Verse 28 of this Thirty-Seventh Psalm shows

Often, the man whom we envy is constantly envying someone else. His greed will not let him rest as long as there is someone in the world that has more than he.

Part of the folly of setting our hearts upon earthly prosperity is the fact that it is so fickle.

that a person who is grasping and greedy will eventually be despised. But people will likely remember a man who has used his means to help others, and his children will be thought of more kindly than will the children of greedy people.

The struggle between the two different kinds of men is brought out in verses 32-34. This struggle started with Cain and Abel and continues to the present time. It is not unusual for the righteous man to be despised by his worldly counterpart. One reason for this is that the life of the one who behaves himself righteously brings condemnation and conviction upon the unwise man. Because he is living by an entirely different value system, the just man is considered to be odd. If he has his goals fixed on an unseen glory, the unsaved man thinks he is mad. All of this stirs hatred in the heart of the wicked, and he plots constantly against the righteous man, for the righteous man seems to be a threat to everything the wicked man stands for. Sometimes, the wicked may even succeed in slaying the righteous, but that is not the end. For God says that in the end He will exalt the righteous (verse 34). When God performs His righteous judgment He will show that the meek man who did not demand his "rights," retaliate against others, or pursue his ends to the hurt of others was right all along. The righteous man will be exalted in the end.

In this regard, read and meditate upon the Beatitudes in Matthew 5.

In verse 35 the psalmist says he has seen the wicked "spreading himself like a green bay tree." But even though the unsaved man may seem to be spreading himself like a tree, he will someday perish. He will be like a dead tree unless he finds the tree of life. The tree of life is that tree upon which the Lord Jesus Christ hung on Cal-

Throughout Scripture the fruitful tree is a symbol of the righteous man (Psalm 1:3).

vary. Only there can life and satisfaction be found in abundance. Only the man who has accepted the salvation paid for on that tree can truly be called "blessed."

NOW TEST YOUR KNOWLEDGE

Answer true or false.
1. "Fret" means to "look away."
2. When we envy the wicked we are in danger of becoming like them.
3. When we envy, we become dissatisfied with the Lord's blessings.
4. We should trust the Lord and not necessarily think that He will reward us for it.
5. Our hearts often deceive us so that we do not even realize our true desires.
6. To "commit" means that we look around to see what everyone else is doing before we start out in a certain direction.
7. Resting is the opposite of fretting.
8. The righteous will not have anything on this earth, but will have it all in Heaven.
9. People will be more apt to love and care for the children of the righteous man.
10. In Scripture, the tree is usually a picture of the wicked.

FOOD FOR THOUGHT

"God's children seem to think that they are no better off than the men of the world. And, according to their faith, so it is done unto them."
—F. B. Meyer

Bow Down
Before Him

LESSON SCRIPTURE
Psalms 15; 103

RELATED SCRIPTURE
Psalms 63; 81; 95; 122; 135

LESSON AIM
To be truly prepared to worship God.

LEARN BY HEART
"For as the heaven is high above the earth, so great is his mercy toward them that fear him. As far as the east is from the west, so far hath he removed our transgressions from us" (Psalm 103:11,12).

8

EVERY DAY WITH THE WORD

Monday	Good works	James 2
Tuesday	The tongue	James 3
Wednesday	God's faithfulness	Psalm 63
Thursday	Deliverance	Psalm 81
Friday	Worship	Psalm 95
Saturday	The right way	Psalm 15
Sunday	God's benefits	Psalm 103

STUDENT'S NOTEBOOK

This column is for the student who desires additional study of the lesson theme.

LESSON PREPARATION

The Wallace family had a terrible time one Sunday morning. The small children had lost their shoes, and teenage Sharon was still drying her hair when it was time to leave the house to attend church. Saturday night activities had left the whole family tired and haggard. Numerous school

Worship on the Lord's Day is important enough to prepare for it all week.

and social activities had left little time for sleep, and the temptation to sleep a little later on Sunday morning had been irresistible. By the time the family had finally arisen, it was too late for breakfast and a hasty cup of coffee had to be worked into the frantic preparation for Sunday School and church.

One word had led to another until finally the entire family was embroiled in a quarrel. By the time the family auto finally turned into the church parking lot, bitterness and chilling quiet had killed any chance of a warm, expectant attitude toward the anticipated worship of the church where they attended. Inside, each family member went to his age group and met friends with a warm smile. But they all had difficulty concentrating upon the Bible lesson. The music and message of the worship service that followed had little effect upon any of them, and they returned to a Sunday afternoon at home exhausted and empty. They had failed to adequately prepare for some of life's most important moments, the time spent at worship. In Psalms 15 and 103, we see some principles applying to both preparation for and practice of worship.

PREPARATION FOR WORSHIP
(Psalm 15)

One of the functions of the public worship service, as well as the teaching time in our churches, is to give us a welcome contrast between the profane, secular world we live in and the vitality of our Christian faith. Properly done, our practice of worship will arm us for the rest of

"Fellowship" is a parallel relationship. It involves two

the week by reinforcing our faith, drawing us closer to God, providing the exhortation we need to act properly and giving us the fellowship of others of like belief. Such results are important to our spiritual well-being and should be properly prepared for. Just as the preacher and teacher prepare their hearts to share the Word of God with us, we would benefit more if our hearts were prepared to receive their message. Spending some moments in prayer and spiritual anticipation for the worship service would be an excellent aid to our time spent in worship. Whether we are engaging in the public worship services or the private act of worship, Psalm 15 lists some things we can do in preparation for worship.

A careful reading of the lesson text will reveal that there are both positive and negative preparations for worship. The psalmist asks a question in verse 1 about what kind of person will draw near to God. Then verse 2 answers with a list of requirements that have to do with the worshiper's walk, his work and his words. His *walk* has to do with his general manner of living. Throughout the week, it is wise to keep in mind the necessity of worshiping God and to let it guide our activities. Our walk should be "upright," or correct.

Our *work* has to do with the major emphasis of our activities. The one who is prepared for worship is the one whose work is righteous, or in accord with God's revealed way. Our words also have a bearing upon our worship, and the prepared worshiper has spoken "the truth in his heart" (verse 2). Our worship is centered around the truth, and it is difficult for the heart that has been living in an unreal and untruthful world to adjust itself to worship in truth (see John 4:23).

people striving together in the same direction or for the same cause. That is the use of the word as it applies to our New Testament assemblies.

"Truth" cannot be divorced from true worship. No matter how sincere, if a group is not centered in the Truth, it cannot be pleasing to God.

In both private and public worship, we are thinking of associations with the ideal Person and the right kind of people. Our associations, therefore, become a part of our preparation for worship. While we will not wish to insulate ourselves from others who need us, our approval should be only upon those whose lives please the Lord. Psalm 15:4 gives that as another proper preparation for worship. Our faithfulness to our commitments is another positive prerequisite given to us in verse 4: "He that sweareth to his own hurt, and changeth not." One of the areas in which Christians are most vulnerable to criticism by the world is in following through on business commitments. If we have been crooked with the world, it is difficult to be straight in our worship.

See II Timothy 2:22.

Remember when "a man's word was his bond"? Christians need to restore that quality to life.

The psalm also contains a number of negative requirements for worship, in verses 3 and 5. "Backbiting" is the cowardly practice of saying about others what we are unwilling to discuss with them in person. Probably no practice so militates against true worship. John, the "apostle of love," asks the question, "For he that loveth not his brother whom he hath seen, how can he love God whom he hath not seen?" (I John 4:20). If we cannot draw near to one whom we can see, how can we draw near with a true heart to One whom we cannot see?

Psalm 15:3 also warns against doing evil to a neighbor. Jesus tells us that we are to do good even to our enemies. And we are not to take up a reproach against a neighbor. Taking up a reproach involves taking sides in a dispute concerning another. The true worshiper is to be a peacemaker, not a participant in conflict (Matthew 5:9). Whenever conflict is necessary, it

Read Luke 10.

should be to defend the truth of God's Word or to protect against danger. To participate in issues over personal rights often leaves the believer open for just criticism and interferes with his capacity for worship by introducing bitterness and strife.

In Psalm 15:5, the psalmist gets into the matter of money. The true worshiper is warned not to profit unduly from those less fortunate than he by "putting out his money to usury. . . ." Although there is a legitimate place for making money off our capital, unjust credit systems have become a great hindrance to worship. Many are not free to worship because they are in bondage financially. And we must admit that our modern credit picture is one of excesses and extreme misuse.

Taking "reward against the innocent" probably refers to the practice of collecting bounty for the apprehension of a party accused of a crime, though not guilty. Any means of profiting from the disadvantage of an innocent party will apply to the warning.

It is only when our lives are right with the God we worship and others around us that we can be properly prepared to worship God acceptably. The believer should do everything in his power to bring his life up to the proper plane of worship. The rewards are well worth the effort. After all, what a privilege it is to be in the presence of the Creator of the universe!

We must be careful not to impose an unrealistic standard upon the teachings of the Bible. Some of the things we call "good business" may merely be ruthless financial advantage.

PRACTICE OF WORSHIP
(Psalm 103)

"How can I bless the Lord?" the Sunday School student asked his teacher after reading

Psalm 103. "All blessings come from Him. How can we give Him anything?"

The original meaning of the word *bless* has to do with an expression of favor made by speech. We can bless the Lord by expressing our love and worship to Him through what we say. It is an act of worship. While we ordinarily think of a blessing as something good that happens, the root of God's blessings upon us lies in the promises that He made in our favor. Through worship, we return our praise to Him for the blessings He has bestowed upon us.

David, the writer of Psalm 103, uses the expression "bless the Lord" five times in this psalm. Twice, he exhorts his own soul to bless the Lord. In verses 20-22, he calls upon angels, the host of Heaven and all God's created works to bless the Lord.

In verse 1 he calls upon all his being to bless the Lord, and verse 2 contains an exhortation not to forget all His benefits. Those benefits are listed in the next verses of the psalm and form an impressive list. They include: *forgiveness* (verse 3), *healing* (verse 3), *redemption* (verse 4), *lovingkindness and tender mercies* (verse 4), *satisfaction* (verse 5), *renewal* (verse 5), *justice* (verse 6), *revelation* (verse 7), *mercy* (verses 8-11), and *removal of our sins* (verse 12).

Great superlative language is used in describing God's mercy. If we can measure the distance from east to west, we can find our sins. But the distance is infinite. And that is how far He has "removed our transgressions from us" (verse 12). The extent of His mercy that was able to do this for us is described in verse 11. Space is so vast that it cannot be measured, but His mercy is said to be

Both a curse and a blessing are uttered with the mouth, says James (James 3:10).

"Merciful" in verse 8 means "compassionate." "Mercy" in verse 8 means "steadfast loyalty."

69

that deep toward us. Nor can eternity be measured. His mercy to us is of an infinite duration, for it is "from everlasting to everlasting" (verse 17). David stretches the limits of language to express his gratitude to God for what He has done. Surely, there is no more worthy use of our imagination than to meditate upon and to express the far reaches of His limitless blessings toward us (see Ephesians 3:18,19).

A touching description of God's feeling toward us is found in Psalm 103:13-17. Verse 13 tells us that His pity is like that of a father. As a father would grow tenderhearted in realizing the inability, infirmity and weakness of his son, so our Heavenly Father pities us. His anger does not burn toward us when we stumble in our weakness, "for he knoweth our frame; he remembereth that we are dust." Our ability is not as important to Him as His mercy toward us.

The word "pitieth" in verse 13 is the same as "merciful" in verse 8—it is literally "compassionate" or "has compassion."

We see in verses 15,16 that we cannot depend upon our own strength. While God is high and exalted, we are as the grass. Our glory fades like a fading flower and our importance as a blade of grass.

Our role in this is found in verses 17,18. His mercy is toward those who "fear him," "keep his covenant," and "remember his commandments to do them." We are weak and faltering in our walk and work. But His mercy ("steadfast loyalty") toward us is based in His covenant promises. To the New Testament believer, the covenant is in Christ and faith in His shed blood.

The last characteristic of God in this list is found in verse 19. We bless Him and worship Him because He is over all. He is the Ruler, the King who has prepared His throne in the heavens. We

"Worship" comes from an old English word that used to be rendered "worthship." We worship God because of His worth. He is the only one worth worshiping.

lift our blessings and our worship to the One who is higher than the heavens! His exalted position is over the angels, over the stars and over all the works of His hands.

When the believer draws near to worship, it is with the realization that he is approaching One whose Person is not only full of mercy and goodness toward us, but who is so mighty and so powerful that His very attributes demand our praise.

FOOD FOR THOUGHT

What greater calamity can fall upon a nation than the loss of worship?

NOW TEST YOUR KNOWLEDGE

Answer true or false.

1. It is not necessary to prepare for a worship service since we have people to handle it for us.
2. There are both positive and negative requirements for worship.
3. The people with whom we associate have an effect upon our worship.
4. It is difficult to worship acceptably if we have not been faithful to our commitments to other people.
5. We should take up a reproach against neighbors when they are wrong.
6. There is no way we can bless God, since He already has everything.
7. God blesses with His promises.
8. God's mercy is finite and its extent can be measured.
9. God pities us.
10. When we worship, we should not think of God as being high and mighty.

God's Boundless Patience

LESSON SCRIPTURE
Psalm 78:1-41

RELATED SCRIPTURE
Psalm 79; Romans 2:4; 8:23-31; James
5:1-11

LESSON AIM
To instill in our children, by precept and
example, an appreciation of God's
gracious dealings with us.

LEARN BY HEART
"But he, being full of compassion, forgave
their iniquity, and destroyed them not:
yea, many a time turned he his anger
away, and did not stir up all his wrath"
(Psalm 78:38).

EVERY DAY WITH THE WORD

Monday	A father's responsibility	Ephesians 5:25—6:4
Tuesday	Wicked workers	Psalm 79
Wednesday	God at work	Romans 8:23-31
Thursday	The rich life	James 5
Friday	No hiding	Romans 2
Saturday	Teaching God's words	Deuteronomy 4
Sunday	Worthy of praise	Psalm 33

STUDENT'S NOTEBOOK

This column is for the
student who desires
additional study of
the lesson theme.

LESSON PRESENTATION

There had been a time when the Jordan family
would talk, but now the father of the family, Bill
Jordan, wondered if they would ever have an
opportunity to communicate as they once did.
Now that their three children were getting older, it

seemed that the myriad of activities planned by the school, the church and the community prevented the entire family from ever being home at one time. When they were home, everything seemed so hectic that nobody ever really had time to spend time together.

Bill wondered about the effects of television and the children's peers. He was also concerned about the effect that the secular classroom would have on the children and their faith. He kept wanting to look through some of their textbooks and meet some of their teachers, but there just didn't seem to be any time. The constant demand of evening activities had long since broken up their family altar. But Bill knew that somehow he had to come to grips with the problem of handing down the right kind of convictions to his kids and guiding their faith. After reading the Seventy-Eighth Psalm, he came to realize that it was not the responsibility of the school or the church. It became clear that God had given that responsibility to the father of each family.

GOD'S PLAN FOR THE PEOPLE
(Psalm 78:1-22)

The basic unit of any society is the family. It provides the earliest and best authority structure, the simplest unit of order for survival and the simplest and most enduring picture of our relationship with our heavenly Father. God's plan for the survival of any society is not vested in the state, or even in the church. It is in the first and primary institution, the home. A church is only as strong as the family units that comprise it. A church could not function properly if it were all

Christians need to take the Bible side of the issue now raging over whether the parents or the state have the ultimate responsibility of rearing the children.

While many today are minimizing the importance of the family, Bible-believing people ought to be maximizing its importance.

73

men, all women, or all young people. Government would be meaningless if it did not preside over families.

As far as passing along the truth is concerned, the responsibility is given to the fathers to teach the truth to each succeeding generation. They may build their institutions and support their churches, but in both the Old and New Testaments it is clear that the fathers are given the responsibility of this task of teaching their children (see Ephesians 6:4).

Psalm 78:1-8 outlines this plan. In verse 1, it appears that the word "law" is not being used of the moral law of God, but of a teaching or instruction that God gives to succeeding generations. Although verse 2 has a Messianic fulfillment, its application is that the dark sayings of old must be taught by the fathers (verse 3). The responsibility of the present generation is given in verse 4: "We will not hide them from their children, shewing to the generation to come the praises of the Lord." The plan is repeated in verse 5, and the purpose is stated again in verse 6: "That the generation to come might know them, even the children which should be born; who should arise and declare them to their children."

The matter is presented very clearly here. If the fathers of one generation do not feel the responsibility of passing the truth of God down to the next generation, it likely will not be done. Not every man is called to preside over a congregation as a pastor, but a man faithful to teach his children who, in turn, teach their children, has presided over a sizable congregation in just a few generations.

The example given in Psalm 78 has to do with

As was the case with Israel, the influence of God's blessings and His truth upon the early roots of our own society is a powerful tool for reinforcing the reality of God in the lives of our children.

One good project for families is to plan ways in which their leisure hours can count for God. Taking a spiritually needy person on an outing, using recreation to witness to neighbors, ministering to those who are less fortunate, and many other projects may be taken up.

the mighty dealings of God with the generation which came out of Egypt under Moses and wandered in the wilderness for 40 years, finally resulting in a new generation reaching the promised territory. The negative example is given in verse 8: "And might not be as their fathers, a stubborn and rebellious generation; a generation that set not their heart aright, and whose spirit was not stedfast with God." The following historical example, given in the balance of the Psalm, was to be repeated by each succeeding generation so that they might not be as the generation that was overthrown in the wilderness. This psalm was sung or chanted by the Jews for centuries, and orthodox Jewish congregations still use it as a hopeful buffer against the same kind of thing occurring again.

In verses 9, 10, an example is used of a failure of courage in the day of battle because they had gotten away from the law of God. It is characteristic of a nation that when it loses its moral and spiritual strength it loses its courage. The reason for this loss of courage is given in verse 11. Israel had simply forgotten what God had done in their behalf in the past.

The miracles under Moses are cited in verses 13-16 as the thing the people should have remembered. A frequent error is thinking that the sight of great miracles produces faith. This is not necessarily true. The Jews described here were witnesses to the most greatly known miracles that had ever taken place. Most of the miracles of Elijah and Elisha, as well as those of Jesus and the apostles, were to individual people and not widely known. But the miracles these Jews witnessed were on a gigantic scale, affecting an entire country and millions of people. In spite of the fact that

See the definition of faith in Hebrews 11:1.

God divided the sea (verse 13), stood the water up as a wall (verse 13), led them with a cloud by day and a column of fire by night (verse 14), and brought water out of the rock (verses 15,16), a whole generation perished in the wilderness because of their unbelief. Since "faith cometh by hearing" (Romans 10:17) there is actually more to be gained by handing down the divine record to a generation than if they witnessed the miracles themselves.

After witnessing all of His miracles, that wicked generation in Psalm 78 still asked the unbelieving question in verse 19—"Can God furnish a table in the wilderness?" The Psalmist David was able to say in Psalm 23:5 that He could, but this poor multitude could not say that even in view of the fact that they had witnessed such miracles. We need to teach the very example of their unbelief to our children as a warning. Indeed, this is why God has preserved the record for us.

God's anger was vented on Israel again and again as they murmured against Moses, complained against God and questioned His power. The reason for their judgment is given in verse 22: "Because they believed not in God, and trusted not in his salvation."

See Matthew 6:25-34 where Jesus warns us about undue anxiety about the provision of food and drink. The idea is that preoccupation with the material often supplants our faith.

GOD'S PATIENCE UPON THE PEOPLE (Psalm 78:23-41)

Regardless of the fact that He had to deal harshly with Israel as a warning to succeeding generations, God was longsuffering toward them and did not make a full end of them. The next section of Psalm 78 reveals His abundant patience. When they murmured about the lack of food, He sent them manna. But even though they ate "angel's food" they still complained. He sent them quail, but judged many of them for their hardness of heart and unbelief, striking them with a plague while the meat was still in their mouths. He mixed compassion and mercy with judgment, but nothing seemed to have an effect upon that stubborn generation.

One cannot help but compare this with God's manifold blessings upon western civilization. The more a society is blessed, the more it is required that they recognize the goodness of God. The increasing secularization of our society, along with the alarming decrease in moral values is an indication that we have misused our bounty. There is a disturbing tolerance for immorality even in our Bible-centered churches. God is not going to be pleased if we use our endowed plenty and our new leisure to sin against Him.

See Romans 2:4.

One of the things about which we can be warned is that we ought to reestablish the old values in the home. The value of studying Psalm 78 is to warn us of the consequences that might come about if we do not put the Bible and prayer back into the home, and begin to put God before the other values and activities that have taken His place. Chances are that we will not see a genuine spiritual revival unless we see it taking place in the homes.

Because His goodness to Israel was unappreciated, God had to resort to harsh measures. "When he slew them, then they sought him: and they returned and enquired early after God." That statement in verse 34 contains an ominous warning. If we do not turn to Him because of His goodness, He may have to judge us. And our turning to Him must be genuine. In verses 36,37 we learn that the repentance of Israel was not genuine, "For their heart was not right with Him" (verse 37). God is not pleased with half-hearted religion.

The hope that His blessings will be upon our children is found in verses 38-41. It is found in His patience. We learn first that He is "full of compassion" (verse 38). It is His love to which we appeal. Although He cannot excuse our sin, we can come to Him for mercy on the basis of our faith in Him. Our children need to learn that, although God is a God of justice, this is not all He is. They need to know that He loves them, and they can learn that love firsthand from their fathers. The primary responsibility for showing love in the home is given to the husband and father (Ephesians 5:25).

We also see His *forgiveness* in verse 38. He is "faithful and just to forgive us our sins" (I John 1:9). So that they will not be overcome with guilt, our children need to know that forgiveness is abundantly available if they will meet His requirements for it. It has been pointed out that many of the excesses of our day arise from a massive guilt complex. That is not necessary if we would only avail ourselves of the forgiveness of God.

Another discovery in Psalm 78:38 is His *patience*. It is true that "many a time turned he his anger away." If it were not for the patience and longsuffering of God, we might all have been consumed. But He understands our infirmities and weaknesses. He "remembered that they were but flesh." Far from seizing upon this as a license

The second coming of Christ was being used by the Thessalonian Christians as an excuse for not applying themselves. Can we sometimes be guilty of letting it interfere with our proper concern for the next generation?

to sin, we ought to see it as a reason for loving Him more, and therefore serving Him better.

The wilderness generation "limited the Holy One of Israel" (verse 41). They did not fully realize the extent of His power. Could it be that the future of our society depends upon this generation of fathers rehearsing in the ears of their children the power of God? Are we depending more upon human strength than we are upon His strength? This is an urgent question to ponder at this time.

FOOD FOR THOUGHT

"Many a son has lost his way among strangers because his father was too busy to get acquainted with him."

—William Brownell

NOW TEST YOUR KNOWLEDGE

Answer true or false:

1. Teaching children about life is a responsibility that God has given primarily to the school and the church.
2. Unborn generations are not our problem.
3. Jews were to remind their children of the stubbornness and rebellion of their fathers.
4. Morality has nothing to do with courage.
5. Our faith would grow stronger if we could observe miracles as Israel did in Egypt.
6. Our children should be taught that God is longsuffering.
7. We can safely compare the history of Israel with the history of western civilization.
8. God's goodness brought Israel to its senses, but His acts of judgment never had that effect.
9. The primary responsibility for showing love in the home is given to the mother.
10. In His dealings with us, God takes into account our weaknesses.

Keep The Way Clear

10

LESSON SCRIPTURE
Psalms 32; 51

RELATED SCRIPTURE
Psalms 6; 38; 102; 130; 143

LESSON AIM
To confess sin promptly and sincerely.

LEARN BY HEART
"The sacrifices of God are a broken spirit:
a broken and a contrite heart, O God, thou
wilt not despise" (Psalm 51:17).

EVERY DAY WITH THE WORD

Monday	Sin	Psalm 51
Tuesday	Weakness	Psalm 6
Wednesday	Suffering	Psalm 38
Thursday	Hope	Psalm 102
Friday	Redeemer	Psalm 130
Saturday	Helper	Psalm 143
Sunday	Forgiveness	Psalm 32

**STUDENT'S
NOTEBOOK**

This column is for the
student who desires
additional study of
the lesson theme.

LESSON PREPARATION

As a young man, David, the son of Jesse, had
killed a lion and a bear to protect the flock he kept.
Later, as King Saul and the whole Israeli army
shuddered in fear, he met the challenge of the
Philistine champion, the giant, Goliath, and sub-
dued him with the shepherd sling. The women had
sung, "Saul hath slain his thousands, and David
his ten thousands," in recognition of his feats as a
warrior (I Samuel 18:7). He had successfully

withstood the attempts of King Saul upon his life, even sparing the life of his enemy on two different occasions. In all the annals of greatness, there is no mightier warrior than David.

But the king who had conquered in many other battles was defeated upon the rooftop by his deadliest and most subtle enemy, sin. The record was given to us to warn us. We fancy ourselves as strong, able to handle things, mighty in battle. But the enemy we often face in our own hearts will defeat us if we are not careful.

Study carefully James 1:12-15. "Lust" means simply "desire."

Thankfully, there is forgiveness and cleansing with God. In Psalms 51 and 32 we have the opportunity to observe some definite principles of God's forgiveness.

THE SAINT REQUESTING FORGIVENESS (Psalm 51)

Mercy is the ground of forgiveness. We find our resource in the mercy of God. David saw the mercy of God in meeting sin described by three different terms in Psalm 51:1,2— "transgression," "iniquity," and "sin." We can picture our own sins in the meaning of these three words, which are used throughout the Bible.

"Transgression" is a word that has to do with our rebellion against God and breaking of His commandments. He marks out our course, which is a good course, but we "transgress" or go beyond it. He means to show us the good way, but we take matters into our own hands and mark out our own way. David asks that his transgressions be "blotted out." He appeals to the mercy of God to remove the record of them. In Colossians 2:14

See James 2:9-11. God's law is a unit.

82

we learn that this is done for us by the blood of Christ.

The word "iniquity" means "crookedness." It is the life that is consistent and straight that God desires for us. Nowadays, it is unfashionable, even in many Christian circles, to be called "straight." But realizing that his life has taken a crooked turn, David wants to be thoroughly washed from his iniquity. The original word for "wash" speaks of scrubbing vigorously in order to remove a deep stain. Our iniquities leave a stain in our consciences, our reputations and our emotions. The guilt can be "thoroughly cleansed" only by the blood of Jesus Christ (I John 1:7-9).

The third word David uses in connection with his wrongdoing is the word "sin." This speaks of David's specific act of transgression against God—his adultery with Bathsheba. For this sin, David seeks a cleansing, a pure heart. David does not once ask for a removal of God's righteous judgment, but requests purity and restoration. He recognizes the fact of his sin. This is a difficult thing to do, but it is necessary if we are to receive the blessing of God (see Proverbs 28:13).

It is a difficult matter to deal properly with the seriousness of our own sin. We often make light of it, or flippantly acknowledge it. But to see it in its true perspective is a rare thing for a man to do. One of the things that underscores its seriousness is that it is an offense to a holy God. David admits this in Psalm 51:4. He acknowledges that his sin was an affront to God.

When the matter of sin is brought up, we often say, "But, you see, this is the reason. . . ." We open our mouths to make excuse. But in Romans 3:19, we read that the law speaks so "that every

"His cross, His blood, His righteousness—my only hope, my plea. My sins deserved eternal death, but Jesus died for me."

mouth may be stopped, and all the world may become guilty before God." David had seen himself guilty before God.

The depravity of man is taught in Psalm 51:5. That he was born a sinner is made clear. The psalmist was not saying that his mother sinned in conceiving him, but that he took on the nature of Adam from the time of conception.

See Romans 5:12-19. Since, genetically, we were all present in Adam, we all sinned in Adam.

Sin springs forth from the heart, not from the outer circumstances, so David pleads in verses 6,7 for a cleansing in the "inward parts." Hyssop was the bush used to sprinkle the blood on the lintels and doorposts at the first passover in Egypt, and it was later used to sprinkle the blood of the sacrifices in the temple. It speaks of the shedding of blood and ultimately was satisfied by the sacrifice of Christ, which alone can cleanse the heart.

See Jeremiah 17:9 and James 1:13-15. These verses give God's accurate diagnosis of what we are like apart from His grace.

The "broken bones" in verse 8 are probably a reference to the practice of oriental shepherds. When a lamb is a habitual stray, the shepherd breaks a leg to teach him not to wander. While the leg is broken, the lamb must stay close to the shepherd for protection. David, the shepherd boy, understood this well. He had strayed, and the Lord "broke his leg" to teach him to stay close to God.

In verses 13-16, David makes some promises to God. He is telling God that he can teach what he knows or experiences. If God forgives him, he can then teach others that same truth. David is not offering these things as payment for "services received" from the Lord, but as a thanksgiving offering. "Then will I teach transgressors thy ways" (verse 13); "My tongue shall sing aloud of thy righteousness" (verse 14); and "my mouth shall shew forth thy praise" (verse 15). Each of

Do you teach others about God's forgiveness, love and care from firsthand experience? Let the redeemed of the Lord say so.

us, having been cleansed and restored by God, should do no less than these three things.

In David's time, of course, the practice was to bring an animal as an offering for sin. But King David recognized that the animal offering was meaningless without another kind of sacrifice, which we see in verse 17: "The sacrifices of God are a broken spirit: a broken and a contrite heart, O God, thou wilt not despise." The word "contrite" means "to be crushed in spirit." If David had not had the proper sorrow for his sin, for him to offer an animal sacrifice would not have been acceptable to God. In offering God the sacrifice of a broken heart, however, the sinner pleases God (verse 19).

See II Corinthians 2:1-7; 7:10. Sorrow itself is not repentance, but sorrow "worketh repentance."

THE SAINT REJOICING IN FORGIVENESS
(Psalm 32)

In Psalm 51, we see the contrite sinner pouring out his heart to God, praying for His forgiveness. In Psalm 32, having received forgiveness, the joyful David is extolling the forgiveness he has received.

To be forgiven is to be happy. It is a release from guilt, a great spiritual windfall. It is one of the most desirable things that could happen to a person, for guilt plagues all of us. And thus David begins the Thirty-Second Psalm, "Blessed is he whose transgression is forgiven, whose sin is covered." The only way sin and guilt can be removed from the life is through the forgiveness of God. Guilt can be psychologically repressed, or the conscience can be seared—but the shame is still there unless God has cleansed the guilty sinner by

See Jeremiah 6:15. We can lose the proper reaction to

His mercy and grace. The happiest man in the world is the man who has had his sin forgiven.

The word "impute" in verse 2 is a bookkeeping term. It means to "account" or "reckon." Our modern word is "compute." When the Lord "imputeth not iniquity" it means that He has removed it from the record. The guilty sinner comes to court only to find that there is no record of his sin. No wonder David calls this man happy!

In verses 3-6 we see the value of confession. To attempt to hide our sin results only in harm to the body and hunger for the soul, as David says in these verses. He reports, "my bones waxed old" and "thy hand was heavy upon me" when he refused to acknowledge his sin. It is only by coming clean with God (verse 5) that we can have relief and cleansing. We are not to be sorry over the consequences of sin, or for being caught. We are to acknowledge the sin itself. God knows about it all the time, but as long as we try to hide it in our own hearts He cannot deal with us in mercy. For us to fail to recognize the seriousness of a sin would only result in constant repetition of that sin even if we did experience forgiveness.

The word "confess" (verse 5) means to "bemoan." It implies a wringing of the hands. When we sin, we should be grieved. We need to realize the seriousness of every sin we commit. We must see sin in the way God sees it so we can deal with it adequately.

Verses 6,7 remind us that in a time of the "floods of great waters," or the trouble that comes into our lives because of sin, God is our only protection. Instead of running *from* Him, we need to run *to* Him and pray for His forgiveness.

In verses 8,9, David pleads for his reader or

shame, given here as the ability to blush, but that does not do away with the shame itself.

I John 1:9

The Prodigal Son returned to his father.

"Self control" as it is used in the New Testament does not imply self-dependence, but rather the ability to instantly recognize and obey the impulses of the Holy Spirit.

The false message of the adversary is that serving God will bring sorrow. Satan would have us believe that it is the way of the saint that is hard, rather than the way of the sinner.

hearer to be sensitive to the lesson involved here. For the believer to be brought to the place where a simple change of expression can bring a response is an illustration of being guided with the eye (verse 8). We can see this in the lives of well-trained children. Beasts, on the other hand, must be trained with the whip and bridle. This is an excellent lesson for us. If we are sensitive to our own sins, to the leading of the Holy Spirit and to the ways of God, we will come to the place where our wills are not so stubborn. We can come to the condition of instant obedience to God, dealing with every shortcoming immediately and keeping good accounts with the Lord.

David sums up his whole appraisal of the joy of forgiveness by saying, "Many sorrows shall be to the wicked: but he that trusteth in the Lord, mercy shall compass him about." The utter joy of having a cleansed heart and life is given in verse 11.

In *Pilgrim's Progress,* Christian was greatly relieved when at last the burden had fallen from his shoulders and he was released from its toil and labor. Such is the case of the one who has experienced God's forgiveness.

FOOD FOR THOUGHT

"The only hope of a sinner when crushed with the consciousness of sin is the mercy of God."
—Albert Barnes

NOW TEST YOUR KNOWLEDGE

Answer true or false:
1. David's lust was a mightier foe than Goliath.
2. God's mercy does not work in our behalf.
3. Transgression arises from our rebellion.
4. "Iniquity" means "straight and narrow."
5. "Sin" in Psalm 51:2 refers to David's pride.
6. Hyssop is a bowl of water.
7. Guilt is not much of a problem with the majority of people.
8. The word "confess" in Psalm 32:5 means "to bemoan."
9. The way of the saint is harder than the way of the sinner.

The Shepherd's Care

11

LESSON SCRIPTURE
Psalm 23

RELATED SCRIPTURE
Psalms 34; 52; 59

LESSON AIM
To commit a specific need to the Good Shepherd's care.

LEARN BY HEART
"Surely goodness and mercy shall follow me all the days of my life: and I will dwell in the house of the Lord forever" (Psalm 23:6).

EVERY DAY WITH THE WORD

STUDENT'S NOTEBOOK

This column is for the student who desires additional study of the lesson theme.

Monday	Blessing	Psalm 34
Tuesday	Ruin	Psalm 52
Wednesday	Protection	Psalm 59
Thursday	Satisfaction	Psalm 23
Friday	Victory	Psalm 27
Saturday	Guidance	John 10
Sunday	Service	Hebrews 10:19-25

LESSON PREPARATION

The reader should resist the temptation to regard this psalm lightly because of its familiarity.

The best known and most beloved song in the entire psalter is Psalm 23. Perhaps the secret of its enduring acclaim is the familiarity with which it presents the relationship of Jehovah with His people. David understood what a shepherd was. The relationship between shepherd and sheep was formed deeply within his mind in the years when, as the youngest son of Jesse, it fell his lot to tend the flock of his father.

As did other oriental shepherds, he no doubt named the sheep, making pets of them. During lonely hours on the Judean hillside, they were his only company. He would talk to them. They came to know his voice as surely as a child would. He would rescue them from the slightest difficulty, protect them from approaching danger and risk his life to chase away the marauding predators that threatened them. He knew where to find a smooth pond of water for them to satisfy their thirst, because sheep will not drink from troubled water. He led them into lush green meadows to feed. And he guided them through the shadowy valleys. All the while, he was meditating upon the Scriptures. So it is natural that these familiar scenes became beautiful pictures of the love and care of Jehovah, and imbedded themselves deeply upon the heart of the shepherd boy who would one day become the king over all Israel and the sweet singer of the Psalms.

WALKING WITH THE SHEPHERD
(Psalm 23:1-3)

The Shepherd Psalm lies in a strategic position. Psalm 22 tells prophetically of the crucifixion of Christ, while Psalm 24 speaks of His Second Coming. In the Twenty-Third Psalm, we see our walk with the heavenly Shepherd. This psalm can be closely compared with John 10, where the Shepherd is identified. In verse 11, Jesus said, "I am the good shepherd: the good shepherd giveth his life for the sheep."

In order to give this familiar psalm additional

Do you have a personal relationship with the Shepherd of Psalm 23 and John 10?

meaning, we have divided it according to divine benefits. In verse 1 we read, "The Lord is my shepherd. . ." That is *divine protection*. One of the main jobs of the shepherd is to protect the flock from danger. As the shepherd faces many of the dangers of his job, he literally lays his life on the line. David himself found it necessary to kill a lion and a bear to protect the sheep.

Our ultimate danger was the loss of our own souls. The Lord Jesus Christ, our Shepherd, met the adversary in the wilderness and upon the cross and defeated him in our behalf. And now He protects us from harm. In order for this protection to be realized, we must understand the importance of the little personal pronoun, "my." We must see the Saviour dying upon the cross as in Psalm 22, and make Him our own personal Saviour in order to enjoy His protection. We must be able to say, "The Lord is my shepherd."

Verse 1 continues, "I shall not want." That is *divine satisfaction*. Once Jesus met a woman deep in sin, at the well of Sychar. Searching for satisfaction, she had already gone through four husbands and was now living with a man who was not her husband. She was a fitting symbol of the way in which the world searches for satisfaction. But Jesus told her, "Whosoever drinketh of the water that I shall give him shall never thirst; but the water that I shall give him shall be in him a well of water springing up into everlasting life" (John 4:14). The world is always saying, "I want." But to the one who walks with the Shepherd, the deepest needs have been supplied, and he can say, "I shall not want."

Those who walk with the Shepherd will find, "He maketh me to lie down in green pastures"

The vacuum in the heart that longs for satisfaction can be filled only with the One for whom it was created—God Himself.

As it is used in Psalm 23:1, "want" means lack. With the Lord as our Shepherd, we lack nothing. He supplies every need, so that we may know full contentment.

(Psalm 23:2). That is *divine accommodation.* For the believer, it is true both in the material and the spiritual sense. Every believer can testify that the heavenly Shepherd has provided for his physical needs. There is a deeper meaning here, however. There can be no true satisfaction unless the heart and the spirit are fed as well. The green pastures are a symbol of the Word of God, from which we feed. We also see this accommodation in the still waters, for water is also a picture of spiritual provision through the Word of God. We do not drink at the troubled fountains of the world's philosophies, but at the quiet stream of God's never-failing truth.

We are reminded in verse 3 that "He restoreth my soul." Here we see *divine restoration.* Everywhere around us we see things failing, decaying, running down. But to the believer there is a never-failing source of renewal. Our redeemed souls are eternal, never growing older, ever being renewed. We have an unfailing fountain of strength in Him.

See II Corinthians 5:17. The "new creation" is not dying as the old one is.

"He leadeth me. . ." In verses 2 and 3 we see *divine direction.* The divine Shepherd is not a far-off influence of some kind who has created the universe and then let it spin itself into oblivion. He is a personal God who is able to give us constant leadership. He leads us through His Holy Spirit, His Word and the counsel and the teaching of other believers. How wonderful it is to be able to go to the God of Heaven for leadership!

God leads us "in the paths of righteousness" (verse 3). This speaks of *divine selection.* "Right- eousness" means "right." He leads us, not in wrong paths, but in the right paths. God said through Solomon, "But the path of the just is as the shining light, that shineth more and more unto the perfect day. The way of the wicked is as darkness: they know not at what they stumble" (Proverbs 4:18,19). When He commands us to walk in a certain way it is because, like the shepherd with the sheep, He knows which path is best for us.

See Psalm 119:105. The Word is the light. Those who do not have the light cannot see their way, and are thus stumbling in the darkness.

God's leadership of the sheep is "for his name's sake" (Psalm 23:3). This is *divine determination*. It is not merely a meandering path with no plot that He charts for us. His path has a purpose. In Ephesians 1:10 we read of God's eternal purpose: "That in the dispensation of the fulness of times he might gather together in one all things in Christ, both which are in heaven, and which are on earth; even in him." It is His purpose that all roads lead to Christ, and all things be done for the glory of His Name. God is remaking us in His own image. He is leading a whole new creation to conform to the image of Christ (Romans 8:29).

TALKING TO THE SHEPHERD (Psalm 23:4-6)

Beginning in verse 4 of Psalm 23, the psalmist is talking directly to the Shepherd. Such is the familiarity that we enjoy with Him.

"Yea, though I walk through the valley of the shadow of death, I will fear no evil: for thou art with me" (verse 4). In the heavenly Shepherd, the believer has *divine preservation*. All the dangers and snares that lie along the way have lost their threat. In addition, there is the touching personal reference to the Shepherd—"thou art with me" (verse 4). The heavenly Shepherd has already

"The shadow of death" is a Hebrew idiom meaning "deep darkness," referring to trouble.

93

walked through the valley and knows the way. We need not fear, for He walked the valley for us.

"Thy rod and thy staff they comfort me" (verse 4). This is a picture of *divine correction*. The shepherd will often push, prod and deliver a sharp blow with his rod and staff. All of this is to correct the path of the sheep. We are reminded that the heavenly Shepherd often uses suffering in this life as a reproof to correct our path. But we can even take comfort in His rod and staff, knowing that He always leads us in the right way.

"Thou preparest a table before me in the presence of mine enemies" (verse 5). Here we see *divine provision*. Even when danger threatens and conflict is near, He provides for us. Our table is often filled with the choicest dainties so that our enemies envy us. Even when the enemies of Famine and Hunger stalk the earth, as with Jacob of old, He provides our needs. We can readily claim the promise of Philippians 4:19: "But my God shall supply all your need according to his riches in glory by Christ Jesus."

"Thou anointest my head with oil; my cup runneth over" (Psalm 23:5). The Shepherd is not skimpy in providing for us, but provides abundantly, with *divine profusion*. Oil is a symbol of plenty even today. In Scripture, it is often a symbol of the rich blessings of the Holy Spirit. How often, after a rich spiritual blessing, we have been led to say, "My cup is full!" It is "according to his riches in glory" that He provides for us. Although the world does not understand, it is in the spiritual realm that our blessings are the greatest. He ministers to us abundantly, beyond measure.

"Surely goodness and mercy shall follow me all the days of my life" (verse 6). This is *divine*

The heavenly Shepherd has walked through the valley of the shadow of death ahead of us (see Hebrews 2:14,15).

Some of the things we often think of as needs are not true needs. This is a special problem in an affluent society.

association. The twins of His care, "goodness and mercy," are always with the believer. "Goodness" speaks of His never-failing ability to act toward us in the best possible way. God is always good, no matter what the appearances. "Mercy" is "steadfast loyalty." God never fails nor forsakes us. He is with us even when we forsake and deny Him, prodding us back into the path He has for us.

"And I will dwell in the house of the Lord forever" (verse 6). To end this glorious song in a glorious way, David speaks of a *divine occupation*. Besides providing our every need, protecting us in the midst of deep trouble, guiding us along the path of His choosing, and abundantly blessing us, the Lord allows us to show our thanks to Him by serving Him. "The house of the Lord" refers to the place of worship, and "forever" literally means "length of days"—for the rest of a life. We should never shun or belittle the responsibility and privilege the Lord has given us of serving Him. It is a distinct responsibility, for only those who are redeemed can carry out the work of the Lord. And it is a unique privilege, for only those whom the Lord calls His own can truly show their thanks to Him through their lives. Let us realize the divine inheritance that is ours, and fulfill our responsibility to give Him our entire being to use as He sees fit.

FOOD FOR THOUGHT

"The young lions do lack and suffer hunger: but they that seek the Lord shall not want any good thing" (Psalm 34:10).

NOW TEST YOUR KNOWLEDGE

Answer true or false:

1. David probably got many of the ideas for Psalm 23 while he was a shepherd lad, meditating upon the Scriptures.
2. The position of Psalm 23 in the psalter has nothing to do with its truth.
3. An oriental shepherd was usually reluctant to protect the sheep if it endangered his life to do so.
4. The "green pastures" and "still waters" may both be compared to the Word of God.
5. Our spirits grow old along with our bodies.
6. God's eternal purpose is revealed in Ephesians 1:10.
7. There is no way God can know what it is like to die.
8. God never sends suffering our way to make us change our path.
9. We should never expect that God will send us more than we need.
10. The "house of the Lord" is a literal place, and not a mere figure of speech.

The Secret Place

12

LESSON SCRIPTURE
Psalm 91

RELATED SCRIPTURE
Matthew 23:37-39; Ruth 2:11,12; I Peter 5:6,7; Psalms 47; 105

LESSON AIM
To take refuge in the shadow of the Most High.

LEARN BY HEART
"He shall call upon me, and I will answer him: I will be with him in trouble; I will deliver him, and honour him" (Psalm 91:15).

EVERY DAY WITH THE WORD

Monday	The fruitful life	John 15:1-14
Tuesday	Ready for battle	Ephesians 6:10-18
Wednesday	An entreaty	Psalm 61
Thursday	Exalt the Lord!	Psalm 57
Friday	God's greatness	Psalm 46
Saturday	Our unworthiness	Psalm 90
Sunday	A safe retreat	Psalm 91

STUDENT'S NOTEBOOK

This column is for the student who desires additional study of the lesson theme.

LESSON PREPARATION

Chad always seemed to be up to something. His life reflected a strange, quiet joy. He had something in his life that you could not quite put your finger on. Nothing seemed to shake him. When things went wrong, he would just grin and take them in stride. At the same time, there was an almost electric power about his life. His strength of character and power to meet every challenge without wavering kept an aura of respect all about him. Not everybody agreed with his opinions and convictions, but everybody knew Chad was the real thing.

One by one, as his co-workers asked him how he could take everything so calmly, he would have opportunity to witness to them that he was a Christian. Frequently, other Christians who worked in the plant marveled at Chad's great strength and power for living. Modestly, he would admit that he was really not as strong as he appeared, but that he had a practice of spending a fraction of his day in prayer and quiet meditation on the Bible. Then, throughout the day, he would "practice the presence of God" in his daily walk and life. He based this habit on the first verse of the Ninety-First Psalm: "He that dwelleth in the secret place of the Most High shall abide under the shadow of the Almighty."

A person does not have to be a mystic or a monk to maintain constant communion with God. It can be done even in the midst of the pressing circumstances of life.

THE SECRET SANCTUARY
(Psalm 91:1-8)

You are driving down a lovely side road, approaching a wooded area. A sign beside the road warns motorists that this area is a "bird sanctuary." The law is on the side of the birds in that area, and anyone harming them has to deal with the officials who protect them. It is a place to which the birds can go and remain safe from harm because they are protected.

God has a spiritual sanctuary, but it is not confined to any one geographical area. It is anywhere one of His children wants to draw nigh to Him in the "secret place" of His presence. Most of our difficulties come from experiencing spiritual weaknesses or breaking spiritual laws. We can find abundant protection from such spiritual dangers in the "secret sanctuary" of the soul. God casts the shadow of His protection over us as a hen gathers her chicks under her wings. That is the thought we see before us in Psalm 91:1.

"Saint" and "sanctuary" come from the same root word.

Two words are used here which speak of a settled practice. They are "dwell" and "abide." This does not indicate a frantic rushing to His presence only when danger is imminent, but a habit of life. An occasional visit to the sanctuary does not guarantee protection. It is "dwelling" in the secret place that is important. The believing heart must take up its abode in the very secret place of the "Most High." He must learn to "practice the presence of God."

The world may offer more tempting, immediate sanctuaries in pleasures, finances or other area, but in the face of them all, the psalmist says, "I will say of the Lord, He is my refuge and my fortress: my God; in him will I trust" (verse 2). A "refuge" is a place to which to flee for safety. A "fortress" is a place of strong defense. Both of these ideas are involved in the "secret sanctuary." We have a place to which we may go in time of danger. It is a place that is secure against danger and harm. It is in the very presence of Jehovah.

It requires a definite commitment on our part to name Him as our protection.

See Ephesians 6:10-17. Our armor and our strength are "in the Lord."

There is a striking commentary on this in the book of Philippians: "Be careful [filled with care] for nothing; but in every thing by prayer and supplication with thanksgiving let your requests be made known unto God. And the peace of God, which passeth all understanding, shall keep your hearts and minds through Christ Jesus" (Philippians 4:6,7). The word "keep" involves guarding or garrisoning. Paul was saying essentially the same thing the writer of Psalm 91 says. It is certain that God is a sure refuge. We can commit our souls to Him.

Imagine yourself as a hunter's prey, with snares set everywhere to catch your feet. The traps are not out in the open, but are hidden in a thousand clever ways. Every step is fraught with danger because there is no way of knowing if the next step will find the fowler's [hunter's] snare. The picture of Psalm 91:3 is one of imminent danger. And it is a true picture, since there are spiritual traps laid everywhere about us. Our spiritual walk is constantly taking us into places in which our feet can be caught in Satan's snare. The trap may result in dangers that are more evident, such as financial bondage, ruined health or moral disgrace, but the dangers are spiritual in origin much of the time.

After our soul has been made secure by salvation in Christ, the only hope for the adversary is to trip us in our "walk," our general manner of living.

Imagine, again, that a serious epidemic had invaded the town where you live. In every home and in every public place, there was a chance that you or your family might contract the infectious disease and become fatally ill. The Bible pictures sin as a rampaging epidemic of spiritual and moral leprosy, endangering everyone around. That is the thrust of verses 6,7 in Psalm 91. While all around us, others may be succumbing to the widespread danger and harm, we can find safety and security in the promise, "Surely he shall deliver thee from the snare of the fowler [hunter, trapper], and from the noisome pestilence [raging epidemic]" (verse 3).

The phrase, "under his wings" (verse 4) presents us with an abiding and wonderful picture of Jehovah's compassionate concern and protection, as if a mother hen were protecting her chicks from the threat of present danger.

Freedom from fear is promised us in verses 5,6. This is a need that each of us has, for fear often drives us into foolish decisions and actions.

In attempting to strike courage into his countrymen in World War II, Franklin Roosevelt said, "We have nothing to fear but fear itself." He realized that often the fear of danger is a greater harm than the danger itself. The Lord realizes this, too, so He begins verse 5 with the reassuring words, "Thou shalt not be afraid." We are promised courage in both the day and the night, under every conceivable kind of danger. Neither the spreading epidemic, quietly sending its tentacles through the night, or the heat of destruction at noonday will be able to intimidate or frighten the believer who is in the shadow of Jehovah's protection.

Nor will the weight of numbers make any difference. Verses 7,8 promise that it does not make any difference how many others are being afflicted or destroyed. The circumstances that are reflected in the numbers do not change the ability of God to protect us. He remains constant, and our protection is the same though "a thousand shall fall at thy side, and ten thousand at thy right hand."

Throughout His time on earth, Jesus constantly cautioned His disciples, "Fear not."

THE SECURE SALVATION
(Psalm 91:9-16)

Security is a strong possibility for every believer. We can know, according to Psalm 91, that our lives are secure, bound up in the keeping power of the Lord.

Susan had grown up in an unsatisfactory home situation. Her parents often quarrelled, and their marriage remained uncertain for years, finally ending in a tragic divorce. Her father had been a heavy drinker, and never had provided her with an adequate image as a father. Meanwhile, Susan had come to know the Lord and had married a Christian. As they started their own Christian home, however, it soon became evident that Susan was very insecure. Ghosts of her former home life kept threatening her relationship with her husband as she kept putting pressure upon him to give her both financial and emotional security. One of the lessons Susan needed to learn was that she could find complete security in her home only as she found it in the Lord. She needed to learn also that salvation is not only salvation from the penalty of sin, but deliverance from sickness, danger, poverty and other areas about which she was constantly worrying.

Although it is true that care should be taken about the ordinary dangers of life, we have to admit that worry never changed a single one of them. The Lord, on the other hand, is capable of answering our prayers and giving us deliverance from the harshest of things that may threaten our security. Verses 9,10 remind us that while living in the "secret place" every believer is indestructible until God deems it otherwise. Even if He should make an exception and allow something to touch the life of His trusting child, it is always the best choice. We may have difficulty understanding His choices, but in faith we can understand

Security is one of the deepest needs of the human spirit. What are some ways in which we can violate the commandments of the Lord by seeking security in the wrong places?

that He always knows best. Knowing that His will is perfect and His protection is secure constitutes total security.

Verses 11,12, misused by Satan in the wilderness to tempt our Lord (Matthew 4:6), have a personal application for us. After the temptation in the wilderness, angels came and ministered unto Jesus. We can be sure that God provides angelic protection for us, as well. God sends these heavenly emissaries to watch over His children, and their presence is certain. It is a reassuring thought that representatives of Heaven are here from before His throne to give us protection. They direct our steps (Psalm 91:11), keep us from harming ourselves (verse 12) and even exercise control over nature in our behalf (verse 13).

Jehovah Himself speaks in the last three verses of Psalm 91. He gives two reasons for His favor upon the believer: "Because he hath set his love upon me" (verse 14) and "because he hath known my name" (verse 14). Both are deeply significant. There are many possible things and persons we could choose to love, but because we choose to *love Him,* in obedience to the first commandment, Jehovah grants us His favor. To *know the name of Jehovah* is to understand something of what His name represents. Have we come to the end of ourselves? He is *the God that provides.* Has our health failed? He is *the God that healeth thee.* Do we need a cause for which to live? He is *God our banner.* Is it salvation that we need? He is *Jehovah our righteousness.* His name represents everything we will ever need.

The following promises are ours because of this. The Lord says, "I will deliver him" (verse 14); "I will set him on high" (verse 14); "I will

Young's Analytical Concordance lists 107 references to angels in the Old Testament, 170 in the New Testament. There are 68 occurrences of the word, "angel" in the Book of Revelation alone. The importance of these beings can hardly be overestimated.

The following names of God tell us much about His character: Jehovah-Jireh—the Lord will provide (Genesis 22:14); Jehovah-Rapha—the Lord our Healer (Exodus 15:26); Jehovah-Nissi—the Lord our Banner (Exodus 17:15); Jehovah-Tsidkenu —the Lord our Righteousness (Jeremiah 33:16).

answer him'' (verse 15); ''I will be with him in trouble'' (verse 15); ''I will. . . honour him'' (verse 15). In addition, the closing verse, 16, promises long life, satisfaction and salvation. It would not be much of a blessing to endure a lengthy life and find no satisfaction. But we are promised a long life with satisfaction, and beyond that, His never-ending salvation.

FOOD FOR THOUGHT

Jesus Christ is no security against storms, but He is perfect security in storms.
—Unknown

NOW TEST YOUR KNOWLEDGE

Answer true or false:
1. God has no particular geographic location in which His presence can be known more fully.
2. A ''refuge'' is a place to which we flee for safety.
3. ''Fowler'' means ''snake.''
4. God wants us to live lives in which we constantly fear, so we will be careful.
5. If a great many other people around us are in danger, it means that we ought to be more fearful.
6. A certain amount of worry is helpful.
7. Security is knowing that God's will is perfect and that His protection is sure.
8. The more than 200 references to angels in the Bible are not to be taken too literally.
9. God is ready with special blessings if we love Him and know His name.

Love
and Praises

13

LESSON SCRIPTURE
Psalm 116

RELATED SCRIPTURE
Psalm 27; Psalm 107; Hebrews 13:10-16;
Philippians 4:6,7

LESSON AIM
To praise God at all times, even in
adversity.

LEARN BY HEART
"I will offer to thee the sacrifice of
thanksgiving, and will call upon the name
of the Lord" (Psalm 116:17).

EVERY DAY WITH THE WORD

**STUDENT'S
NOTEBOOK**

This column is for the
student who desires
additional study of
the lesson theme.

LESSON PREPARATION

Donna was a faithful, sincere Christian, but her
life had become filled with trouble. She seemed to
have lost the shining, radiant note of victory that
had been characteristic of her life previously, and
her friends had begun to notice this change. One
day, as her pastor had occasion to talk with her, he

105

tried to counsel her not to languish under her difficulties.

"I realize you have had some pretty trying circumstances lately," he said. "But there are so many things that are right, you don't have to emphasize all the wrong things. It would be good for you to practice the art of thanking God for all the right things He has sent your way. And, realizing that He always knows best, it would be healthy for you to thank Him even for the trials."

A thing is right and true whether we are presently experiencing it or not. It is right to praise the Lord regardless of the state of our emotions.

Donna was not convinced. "But I don't *feel* like being thankful," she countered. "Wouldn't that be dishonest? If I pretend to be thankful without really meaning it, isn't that being a hypocrite?"

Pastor Watson mused for a moment over what she had said. Finally, he asked, "Do you believe a person ought to make a sacrifice to God? Or should a person offer to the Lord only what he doesn't want, rather than giving God the best things?"

The answer was obvious, but Donna still did not understand the application. Her wise pastor went on to say, "You are withholding from God some of the best moments and years of your life by living with a defeated attitude. If you offer to God the 'sacrifice of praise' as taught in Psalm 116, He will be pleased with your offering whether or not your emotions are betraying you. And likely, your emotions will follow suit."

AN UNDYING LOVE
(Psalm 116:1-9)

In this psalm of praise, Psalm 116, David speaks of two attitudes toward God. In verse 1, he

Does true love cease to exist when one's feelings change?

says, "I love the Lord." In verse 10, he testifies, "I believed." In the context of these two attitudes, he offers his song of praise. Praise is characteristic of the Psalms. The last section of the collection, Book V, starting in Psalm 107, rises to the highest crescendo of praise in the entire sacred hymnal.

The background of Psalm 116 is an unusual trial from which the writer was delivered. Our hard circumstances provide some of the most unusual opportunities for God to show His power in our lives. For there can be no victories where there is no battle. Against the dark background of David's helpless situation, there shines the bright sun of Jehovah's deliverance. And that deliverance gives rise to the psalmist's "sacrifice of praise."

The precise nature of the writer's trial is not given to us in this psalm, but its severity is underscored by the vivid language. The words "sorrows" (verse 3), "death" (verse 3), "pains" (verse 3), "trouble" (verse 3), "low" (verse 6), "tears" (verse 8), "falling" (verse 8), "afflicted" (verse 10), are words that speak succinctly of the kinds of hardships we all face. They speak volumes about what David must have felt in his trouble, and each of us could use them to describe periods in our own lives.

It is precisely because his situation was so hard, his own strength so inadequate, that David could say, "I love the Lord, because he hath heard my voice and my supplications" (verse 1). After we have endured the full weight of our own inability to cope, we go to Him in prayer and His deliverance is so welcome that we love Him for it. "Supplications" speaks of rehearsing our needs before God, recognizing our own inadequacy and lack of merit. It is possible that David felt his need so greatly that he cried out audibly in despair, as the word "voice" may indicate.

It is probable that as he prayed, David rehearsed to God some of the past deliverances and thanked Him for them, thus offering unto Him the "sacrifice of praise." In Philippians 4:6 we are taught to offer our supplications "with thanksgiving."

Because of past deliverance David promises, "therefore will I call upon him as long as I live" (Psalm 116:2). It pleases the Lord when we call upon Him rather than taking matters into our own hands.

The word "sorrows" in verse 3 was originally a word meaning "cords" or "bonds." In this case it was the bondage of death itself that circled about David's life (see Hebrews 2:15). Often, the very helplessness of our circumstances works a kind of death in our lives. Hope, happiness and pleasure seem to die for a time. It is when the unseen God steps into this situation to bring deliverance that we love Him for His rescue. But there is a greater deliverance than that. We were in spiritual bondage to a hard master until He brought about our redemption through His Son, the Lord Jesus Christ.

It is often our own wrong choices through lack of understanding that bring us to a place of desperate need. On top of the trouble itself, we chide ourselves with the thought, "How could I have been so foolish?" But there is help, because in Psalm 116:6 we read, "The Lord preserveth the simple." David was apparently seeing that his difficulty was the result of some wrong choices.

Since God looks upon the heart, it is not the excellence of speech that makes a prayer more or less effective (see Romans 8:26).

Satan often accuses us by reminding us that we were foolish in our actions and, therefore, ought to be punished for our stupidity. No matter, for God can overcome even our lack of understanding.

But the wisdom of God was able to overrule David's mistakes, and he praised Him for preserving "the simple."

"Bountifully" is the word the writer of this hymn uses in verse 7 to describe God's dealings with him. Then David tells of three things that were involved in the deliverance which he had experienced. Jehovah had delivered his "soul from death," his "eyes from tears," and his "feet from falling." The first has reference to a deliverance from the very real danger of death in which David had found himself. The second, from his inward grief and sorrow. The third form of deliverance probably refers to his whole life and testimony (see Psalm 37:23,24). David had been totally delivered.

Our "walk," as it is used in the Bible, usually refers to our life here on this earth.

In response to this, the psalmist promises that his feet, delivered from the snare, will now walk in the knowledge of God's constant presence. He says, "I will walk before the Lord in the land of the living" (Psalm 116:9). It is only fitting that our lives should show forth the praise due to the One who has delivered us.

AN UNFAILING FAITH
(Psalm 116:10-19)

The central verse of the Bible is Psalm 118:8: "It is better to trust in the Lord than to put confidence in man." The whole function of the Bible as we apply it to our lives is to bring us to that place of putting confidence in the Lord, rather than in our own abilities or those of other men. And so David starts off this section of Psalm 116, beginning with verse 10, by saying, "I believed, therefore have I spoken."

109

Whether David's words involved someone who betrayed his trust, or whether his words were spoken merely out of anger and frustration, the poet says in Psalm 116:10,11: "I was greatly afflicted: I said in my haste, All men are liars." The passage probably reflects the fact that men could not be trusted to keep their word as God can. It is certainly true that, compared with the truth and faithfulness of God, "all men are liars." David, however, seems to be chiding himself for saying this in haste. His concern may have been over his own anger.

While it is true that all men are liars, it is possible to say a right thing with a wrong spirit. God is concerned not only with <u>acts</u>, but with <u>attitudes</u> as well.

Beginning in verse 12, David asks a question that is answered in the remaining verses of this psalm. The question is, "What shall I render unto the Lord for all his benefits toward me?" David had cried out in his trouble, God had answered, and now the poet in his gratitude wants to give something back to Jehovah. The problem is most enlightening. God is not in any kind of trouble, so we cannot recompense Him in kind by delivering Him. What can we "render" unto Him, therefore? There are no material gifts that we can place into His hands, although we have an obligation to recognize Him with our physical resources by giving to His work. We cannot add anything to His person, since He is complete in Himself.

In "giving" to God we add something, not to His person, but to ours.

The psalmist says he will do the following things to show his gratitude: I will "take the cup of salvation" (verse 13); "call upon the name of the Lord" (verse 13); "pay my vows" (verse 14); and "offer. . . the sacrifice of thanksgiving" (verse 17).

At first, we might think it is strange to "take" as a show of gratitude (verse 13). But in a sense, since God is the source of everything, we can give to Him only by receiving from Him. It is only the insensitive, proud, unthankful heart that refuses to take the cup from His hand. It is an insult to Him to refuse the cup, which is a symbol of His great blessing and fulness.

It is also pleasing to the Lord when we go to Him in prayer, rather than ignore His help. And so the divinely guided writer says he will "call upon the name of the Lord" (verse 13).

In verse 14 David might have been thinking about past times that he made promises to the Lord, promises that remained unfulfilled. The goodness of the Lord has led him to say, "I will pay my vows unto the Lord now in the presence of all His people."

The fourth thing David gave God was the sacrifice of thanksgiving. We reward ourselves with self pity and the indulgence of a bitter spirit when we murmur about our circumstances. On the other hand, when we turn from our bitterness (which is usually secretly against the Lord) and offer unto Him a sacrifice of praise and thanksgiving, it rises up to Him as a sweet smelling sacrifice. The writer of Hebrews said, "By him therefore let us offer the sacrifice of praise to God continually, that is, the fruit of our lips giving thanks to his name" (Hebrews 13:15). Since we cannot place anything material in His hands, it is a thrilling reality to know that we can offer Him the fruit of our lips. Knowing that praise pleases Him, that it brings delight to His heart and that He considers it as an offering before His throne, we have powerful motivation to offer it unto Him.

FOOD FOR THOUGHT

If Christians praised God more, the world would doubt Him less.

—Charles E. Jefferson

NOW TEST YOUR KNOWLEDGE

Answer true or false:

1. Psalm 116 is divided into two sections under the thoughts, "I love," and "I believed."
2. The background of Psalm 116 is a time in which David had enjoyed freedom from trouble.
3. "Supplication" means asking God to provide the things we need.
4. Because He is so busy and so important, God wants us to work out most things ourselves.
5. We cannot expect God to help us when we have made stupid decisions.
6. God's deliverance for David had to do with his soul, his eyes and his feet.
7. David had called all men liars.
8. David wanted to give something to the Lord in recognition of His blessings.
9. We can give to God by taking the cup of His salvation and blessing.
10. God recognizes praise as a sacrifice.